Contents

	PAGE
Use of guidance	3
The Approved Documents	3
Limitation on requirements	3
Materials and workmanship	3
The Workplace (Health, Safety and Welfare) Regulations 1992	4
The Requirements	5
Material change of use	6
Interpretation (Regulation 2)	6
Meaning of material change of use (Regulation 5)	6
Requirements relating to material change of use (Regulation 6)	6
Historic buildings	7
Section 0: General	9
Performance	9
Introduction to provisions	9
Flood risk	9
Land affected by contaminants	10
Authorities that should be notified about contamination	10
Definitions	11
Section 1: Clearance or treatment of unsuitable material	12
Site investigation	12
Unsuitable material	12
Section 2: Resistance to contaminants	14
Introduction	14
Solid and liquid contaminants	15
Risk assessment	15
General concepts	15
Stages of risk assessment	16
Hazard identification and assessment	16
Risk estimation and evaluation	17
Remedial measures	17
Introduction	17
Treatment	18
Containment	18
Removal	18
Risks to buildings, building materials and services	18
Methane and other gases from the ground	19
Introduction	19
Risk assessment	19
Remedial measures	20
Radon	21
Section 3: Subsoil drainage	22
Section 4: Floors	24
Ground supported floors (moisture from the ground)	24
Technical solution	24
Alternative approach	25
Suspended timber ground floors (moisture from the ground)	25
Technical solution	26
Alternative approach	27
Suspended concrete ground floors (moisture from the ground)	27
Technical solution	27
Ground floors and floors exposed from below (resistance to damage from interstitial condensation)	28
Floors (resistance to surface condensation and mould growth)	28
Section 5: Walls	29
Internal and external walls (moisture from the ground)	29
Technical solution	29
Alternative approach	29
External walls (moisture from the outside)	31
Solid external walls	31
Technical solution	31
Alternative approach	32
Cavity external walls	32
Technical solution	32
Alternative approach	32
Cavity insulation	32
Framed external walls	36
Cracking of external walls	36
Impervious cladding systems for walls	36
Technical solution	36
Alternative approach	37
Joint between doors and windows	37
Door thresholds	37

C CONTENTS

	PAGE
External walls (resistance to damage from interstitial condensation)	38
External walls (resistance to surface condensation and mould growth)	38
Section 6: Roofs	39
Roofs (resistance to moisture from the outside)	39
Roofs (resistance to damage from interstitial condensation)	40
Roofs (resistance to surface condensation and mould growth)	40
British Standards referred to	41
Other documents referred to	43
Annex A: Guidance on the assessment of land affected by contaminants	47
References to Annex A	48

DIAGRAMS

1	Distribution of shrinkable clays and principle sulphate/sulphide bearing strata in England and Wales	13
2	Example of a conceptual model for a site showing source–pathway–receptor	15
3	Subsoil drain cut during excavation	23
4	Ground supported floor – construction	25
5	Suspended timber floor – construction	26
6	Suspended floor – preventing water collection	26
7	Typical floors exposed from below	28
8	Damp-proof courses	30
9	Protecting inner leaf	30
10	Protection of wall head from precipitation	31
11	Insulated external walls: examples	33
12	UK zones for exposure to driving rain	34
13	Windows reveals for use in areas of severe or very severe exposure to driving rain	37
14	Accessible threshold for use in exposed areas	38
A1.	The process of managing land affected by contaminants	49

TABLES

		PAGE
1	Volume change potential for some common clays	13
2	Examples of sites likely to contain contaminants	14
3	Examples of possible contaminants	17
4	Maximum recommended exposure zones for insulated masonry walls	35

Use of guidance

THE APPROVED DOCUMENTS

This document is one of a series that has been approved by the First Secretary of State for the purpose of providing practical guidance with respect to the requirements of Schedule 1 to and Regulation 7 of the Building Regulations 2000 (SI 2000/2531) for England and Wales. SI 2000/2531 has been amended by the Building (Amendment) Regulations 2001 (SI 2001/3335), by the Building (Amendment) Regulations 2002 (SI 2002/440), by the Building (Amendment) (No. 2) Regulations 2002 (SI 2002/2871), by the Building (Amendment) Regulations 2003 (SI 2003/2692) and by the Building (Amendment) Regulations 2004 (SI 2004/1465).

At the back of this document is a list of all the documents that have been approved and issued by the Secretary of State for this purpose.

Approved Documents are intended to provide guidance for some of the more common building situations. However, there may well be alternative ways of achieving compliance with the requirements. **Thus there is no obligation to adopt any particular solution contained in an Approved Document if you prefer to meet the relevant requirement in some other way.**

Other requirements

The guidance contained in an Approved Document relates only to the particular requirements of the Regulations which the document addresses. The building work will also have to comply with the Requirements of any other relevant paragraphs in Schedule 1 to the Regulations.

There are Approved Documents which give guidance on each of the Parts of Schedule 1 and on Regulation 7.

LIMITATION ON REQUIREMENTS

In accordance with Regulation 8, the requirements in Parts A to D, F to K and N (except for paragraphs H2 and J6) of Schedule 1 to the Building Regulations do not require anything to be done except for the purpose of securing reasonable standards of health and safety for persons in or about buildings (and any others who may be affected by buildings or matters connected with buildings).

The requirements in Part C address health and safety, and do not seek to protect the building fabric for its own sake. Thus the degree of precautions needed to comply with Part C will be influenced by the intended use of the building. Part C may not apply where it can be demonstrated that it will not serve to increase the protection to the health and safety of any persons habitually employed in the building in question.

Paragraphs H2 and J6 are excluded from Regulation 8 because they deal directly with prevention of the contamination of water. Parts E and M (which deal, respectively, with resistance to the passage of sound, and access to and use of buildings) are excluded from Regulation 8 because they address the welfare and convenience of building users. Part L is excluded from Regulation 8 because it addresses the conservation of fuel and power. All these matters are amongst the purposes, other than health and safety, that may be addressed by Building Regulations.

MATERIALS AND WORKMANSHIP

Any building work which is subject to the requirements imposed by Schedule 1 to the Building Regulations should, in accordance with Regulation 7, be carried out with proper materials and in a workmanlike manner.

You may show that you have complied with Regulation 7 in a number of ways. These include the appropriate use of a product bearing CE marking in accordance with the Construction Products Directive (89/106/EEC)[1] as amended by the CE Marking Directive (93/68/EEC)[2], or a product complying with an appropriate technical specification (as defined in those Directives), a British Standard, or an alternative national technical specification of any state which is a contracting party to the European Economic Area which, in use, is equivalent, or a product covered by a national or European certificate issued by a European Technical Approval issuing body, and the conditions of use are in accordance with the terms of the certificate. You will find further guidance in the Approved Document supporting Regulation 7 on materials and workmanship.

Independent certification schemes

There are many UK product certification schemes. Such schemes certify compliance with the requirements of a recognised document which is appropriate to the purpose for which the material is to be used. Materials which are not so certified may still conform to a relevant standard.

Many certification bodies which approve such schemes are accredited by UKAS.

1 As implemented by the Construction Products Regulations 1991 (SI 1991/1620).

2 As implemented by the Construction Products (Amendment) Regulations 1994 (SI 1994/3051).

Technical specifications

Under Section 1(a) of the Building Act, Building Regulations may be made for various purposes including health, safety, welfare, convenience, conservation of fuel and power, and prevention of contamination of water. Standards and technical approvals are relevant guidance to the extent that they relate to these considerations. However, they may also address other aspects of performance such as serviceability, or aspects which, although they relate to the purposes listed above, are not covered by the current Regulations.

When an Approved Document makes reference to a named standard, the relevant version of the standard is the one listed at the end of the publication. However, if this version has been revised or updated by the issuing standards body, the new version may be used as a source of guidance provided it continues to address the relevant requirements of the Regulations.

The appropriate use of a product which complies with a European Technical Approval as defined in the Construction Products Directive will meet the relevant requirements.

The Office intends to issue periodic amendments to its Approved Documents to reflect emerging harmonised European Standards. Where a national standard is to be replaced by a harmonised European Standard, there will be a co-existence period during which either standard may be referred to. At the end of the co-existence period, the national standard will be withdrawn.

THE WORKPLACE (HEALTH, SAFETY AND WELFARE) REGULATIONS 1992

The Workplace (Health, Safety and Welfare) Regulations 1992 contain some requirements which affect building design. The main requirements are now covered by the Building Regulations, but for further information see Workplace health, safety and welfare. *Workplace (Health, Safety and Welfare) Regulations 1992. Approved Code of Practice L24.* Published by HSE Books 1992; ISBN 0 71760 413 6.

The Workplace (Health, Safety and Welfare) Regulations 1992 apply to the common parts of flats and similar buildings if people such as cleaners and caretakers are employed to work in these common parts. Where the requirements of the Building Regulations that are covered by this part do not apply to dwellings, the provisions may still be required in the situations described above in order to satisfy the Workplace Regulations.

The Requirements

This Approved Document deals with the following Requirements which are contained in the Building Regulations 2000 (as amended by SI 2001/3335, SI 2002/440, SI 2002/2871 and SI 2003/2692).

Requirement	*Limits on application*
Site preparation and resistance to contaminants and moisture	
Preparation of site and resistance to contaminants.	
C1. (1) The ground to be covered by the building shall be reasonably free from any material that might damage the building or affect its stability, including vegetable matter, topsoil and pre-existing foundations.	
(2) Reasonable precautions shall be taken to avoid danger to health and safety caused by contaminants on or in the ground covered, or to be covered by the building and any land associated with the building.	
(3) Adequate subsoil drainage shall be provided if it is needed to avoid:	
(a) the passage of ground moisture to the interior of the building;	
(b) damage to the building, including damage through the transport of water-borne contaminants to the foundations of the building.	
(4) For the purpose of this requirement, 'contaminant' means any substance which is or may become harmful to persons or buildings including substances which are corrosive, explosive, flammable, radioactive or toxic.	
Resistance to moisture	
C2. The floors, walls and roof of the building shall adequately protect the building and people who use the building from harmful effects caused by:	
(a) ground moisture;	
(b) precipitation and wind-driven spray;	
(c) interstitial and surface condensation; and	
(d) spillage of water from or associated with sanitary fittings or fixed appliances.	

MATERIAL CHANGE OF USE

Requirement C1 (2), which addresses resistance to contaminants, is now added to the requirements in Regulation 6 of the Building Regulations 2000 which should be complied with when there are certain material changes of use of buildings. Regulation 6 sets out which parts of Schedule 1 should be complied with when there is a material change of use of the building as defined in Regulation 5. The absence of such a requirement would have meant that occupiers of buildings in areas at risk from contaminants may remain unprotected after the building work to effect the change of use is complete.

In particular, some contaminants can penetrate the floors of buildings such as landfill gas arising from the deposition of waste and vapours from spills of organic solvents and fuel. These contaminants can also migrate laterally from land outside the building. In order to deal with this Requirement C1 (2) now applies to all changes of use that have a residential purpose or provide sleeping accommodation including hotels, i.e. as defined by Regulation 5 (a) to 5 (g) with the exception of 5 (e) public buildings and 5 (j) shops. Other types of buildings are covered by Health and Safety legislation so do not need addressing through the Building Regulations, for example workplace assessment, including radon measurements.

Attention is drawn to the following extracts from the Building Regulations 2000 (as amended by SI 2001/3335, SI 2002/440, SI 2002/2871, SI 2003/2692 and SI 2004/1465).

Interpretation (Regulation 2)

'Room for residential purposes' means a room, or suite of rooms, which is not a dwelling-house or flat and which is used by one or more persons to live and sleep in, including rooms in hotels, hostels, boarding houses, halls of residence and residential homes but not including rooms in hospitals, or other similar establishments, used for patient accommodation.

Meaning of material change of use (Regulation 5)

For the purposes of paragraph 8 (1)(e) of Schedule 1 to the Act and for the purposes of these Regulations, there is a material change of use where there is a change in the purposes for which or the circumstances in which a building is used, so that after the change:

a. the building is used as a dwelling, where previously it was not;
b. the building contains a flat, where previously it did not;
c. the building is used as a hotel or boarding house, where previously it was not;
d. the building is used as an institution, where previously it was not;
e. the building is used as a public building, where previously it was not;
f. the building is not a building described in Classes I to VI in Schedule 2, where previously it was;
g. the building, which contains at least one dwelling, contains a greater or lesser number of dwellings than it did previously;
h. the building contains a room for residential purposes, where previously it did not; or
i. the building, which contains at least one room for residential purposes, contains a greater or lesser number of such rooms than it did previously.

Requirements relating to material change of use (Regulation 6)

1. Where there is a material change of use of the whole of a building, such work, if any, shall be carried out as is necessary to ensure that the building complies with the applicable requirements of the following paragraphs of Schedule 1:

a. in all cases,

B1 (means of warning and escape)
B2 (internal fire spread – linings)
B3 (internal fire spread – structure)
B4 (2) (external fire spread – roofs)
B5 (access and facilities for the fire service)
C1 (2) (resistance to contaminants)
F1 (ventilation)
G1 (sanitary conveniences and washing facilities)
G2 (bathrooms)
H1 (foul water drainage)
H6 (solid waste storage)
J1 to J3 (combustion appliances)
L1 (conservation of fuel and power – dwellings);
L2 (conservation of fuel and power – buildings other than dwellings);

b. in the case of a material change of use described in Regulations 5(c), (d), (e) or (f), A1 to A3 (structure);

c. in the case of a building exceeding fifteen metres in height, B4 (1) (external fire spread – walls);
d. in the case of material change of use described in Regulation 5(a), C2 (resistance to moisture);
e. in the case of a material change of use described in Regulation 5(a), (b), (c), (g), (h) or (i) E1 to E3;
f. in the case of a material change of use described in Regulation 5(e), where the public building consists of or contains a school, E4 (acoustic conditions in schools);
g. in the case of a material change of use described in Regulation 5(c), (d), (e), or (j), M1 (access and use);
h. in the case of a material change of use described in Regulation 5(a), (b), (c), (d), (f) – if it provides new residential accommodation, (g), (h) or (i), C1 (2) (resistance to contaminants).

2. Where there is a material change of use of part only of a building, such work, if any, shall be carried out as is necessary to ensure that:

a. that part complies in all cases with any applicable requirement referred to in paragraph (1) (a);
b. in a case to which sub-paragraphs (b), (d), (e) or (f) of paragraph (1) apply, that part complies with the requirements referred to in the relevant sub-paragraphs; and
c. in the case to which sub-paragraph (c) of paragraph (1) applies, the whole building complies with the requirement referred to in that sub-paragraph; and
d. in the case to which sub-paragraph (g) of paragraph (1) applies:
   i. that part and any sanitary appliances provided in or in connection with the requirements referred to in that sub-paragraph; and
   ii. the building complies with requirement M1 (a) of Schedule 1 to the extent that reasonable provision is made to provide either suitable independent access to the part or suitable access through the building to that part; and
e. in the case to which sub-paragraph (g) of paragraph (1) applies, the whole building complies with the requirement referred to in that sub-paragraph.

Historic buildings

Material change of use or alterations to existing buildings may include work on historic buildings. Historic buildings include:

a. listed buildings;
b. buildings situated in conservation areas;
c. buildings which are of architectural and historical interest and which are referred to as a material consideration in a local authority's development plan;
d. buildings of architectural and historical interest within national parks, areas of outstanding natural beauty and world heritage sites.

The need to conserve the special characteristics of such historic buildings needs to be recognised[3]. In such work, the aim should be to improve resistance to contaminants and moisture where it is practically possible, always provided that the work does not prejudice the character of the historic building, or increase the risk of long-term deterioration to the building fabric or fittings. In arriving at an appropriate balance between historic building conservation and improving resistance to contaminants and moisture it would be appropriate to take into account the advice of the local planning authority's conservation officer.

Particular issues relating to work in historic buildings that warrant sympathetic treatment and where advice from others could therefore be beneficial include the following:

a. avoiding excessively intrusive gas protective measures;
b. ensuring that moisture ingress to the roof structure is limited and the roof can breathe[4]. Where it is not possible to provide dedicated ventilation to pitched roofs it is important to seal existing service penetrations in the ceiling and to provide draught proofing to any loft hatches. Any new loft insulation should be kept sufficiently clear of the eaves so that any adventitious ventilation is not reduced.

---

[3] BS 7913:1998 Guide to the principles of the conservation of historic buildings. Provides guidance on the principles that should be applied when proposing work on historic buildings.

[4] SPAB Information Sheet 4 *The need for old buildings to 'breathe'*, 1986.

In most cases the rate at which gas seeps into buildings, mainly through floors, can be reduced by edge located sumps or sub-floor vents. These are less intrusive than internal sumps or ducts that may involve taking up floors. If flagged floors are taken up the stones should be indexed and their layout recorded to facilitate relaying when work is completed[5].

Radon can be dispersed by ventilation strategies such as positive pressurisation. These systems can often be accommodated in an unobtrusive manner.

If internal mechanical ventilation is used to disperse ground gases, it may affect the functioning of combustion appliances and may lead to the spillage of products of combustion into the building. Guidance on this can be found in Good Building Guide 25 Buildings and radon[6].

---

[5] BRE Report BR 267 *Major alterations and conversions: a BRE guide to radon remedial actions in existing buildings*, 1994.

[6] BRE GBG 25 *Buildings and radon*, 1996.

Section 0: General

PERFORMANCE

C1

0.1 In the First Secretary of State's view the requirements of C1 will be met by making reasonable provisions to secure the health and safety of persons in and about the building, and by safeguarding them and buildings against adverse effects of:

a. unsuitable material including vegetable matter, topsoil and pre-existing foundations;

b. contaminants on or in the ground covered, or to be covered, by the building and any land associated with the building; and

c. groundwater.

C2

0.2 In the First Secretary of State's view the requirements of C2 will be met if the floors, walls and roof are constructed to protect the building and secure the health and safety of persons in and about the building from harmful effects caused by:

a. moisture emanating from the ground or from groundwater;

b. precipitation and wind-driven spray;

c. interstitial and surface condensation; and

d. spillage of water from or associated with sanitary fittings and fixed appliances.

INTRODUCTION TO PROVISIONS

0.3 Sections 1, 2 and 3 of this document cover Requirement C1 and deal with site preparation and resistance to contaminants under the headings 'Clearance or treatment of unsuitable material', 'Resistance to contaminants' and 'Subsoil drainage'. Building Regulations are made for the purposes of securing the health, safety, welfare and convenience of persons in and about buildings. This means that action may need to be taken to mitigate the effects of contaminants within the land associated with the building as well as protecting the building and persons in and about the building.

0.4 Hazards associated with the ground may include the effects of vegetable matter including tree roots. They may include health hazards associated with chemical and biological contaminants, and gas generation from biodegradation of organic matter. Hazards to the built environment can be physical, chemical or biological. Items such as underground storage tanks or foundations may create hazards to both health and the building. Physical hazards also include unstable fill or unsuitable hardcore containing sulphate.

0.5 In addition, the naturally occurring radioactive gas radon and gases produced by some soils and minerals can be a hazard.

0.6 Sections 4, 5 and 6 of this document cover Requirement C2 and deal with resistance to moisture under the headings 'Floors', ' Walls' and 'Roofs'. Moisture can rise from the ground to damage floors and the base of walls on any site, although much more severe problems can arise in sites that are liable to flooding. Driving rain or wind-driven spray from the sea or other water bodies adjacent to the building can penetrate walls or roofs directly, or through cracks or joints between elements, and damage the structure or internal fittings or equipment. Surface condensation from the water vapour generated within the building can cause moulds to grow which pose a health hazard to occupants. Interstitial condensation may cause damage to the structure. Spills and leaks of water, in rooms where sanitary fittings or fixed appliances that use water are installed (e.g. bathrooms and kitchens), may cause damage to floor decking or other parts of the structure.

0.7 The diagrams in this Approved Document have been set out to show typical situations and relationships between adjacent elements of construction. Conventional notations and hatching have been used to identify different materials. **However, the diagrams cannot show specific situations. It remains the responsibility of the designer and builder to ensure that the building work meets all relevant aspects of the Building Regulations.**

Flood risk

0.8 There is a presumption in planning guidance[7] that development should not take place in areas that are at risk of flooding. Flood resistance is not currently a requirement in Schedule 1 of the Building Regulations 2000. However, when local considerations necessitate building in flood prone areas the buildings can be constructed to mitigate some effects of flooding such as:

a. elevated groundwater levels or flow of subsoil water across the site – this can be alleviated by the provision of adequate sub-soil drainage (see Section 3);

b. sewer flooding due to backflow or surcharging of sewers or drains – this can be addressed through the use of non-return valves and anti-flooding devices (see Section 3, paragraph 3.6);

[7] Planning Policy Guidance Note PPG 25 *Development and flood risk*, DTLR, 2001.

c. intrusion of groundwater through floors – this can be addressed through the use of water resistant construction (see Section 4, paragraphs 4.7 to 4.12);

d. entry of water into floor voids – provision to inspect and clear out sub-floor voids can be considered (see Section 4, paragraph 4.20).

Further information on flood resistant construction can be found in a number of publications[8–10].

Land affected by contaminants

0.9 The guidance given on resistance to contaminants in Section 2 is for the purposes of the Building Regulations and their associated requirements. Users of this document should be aware that there may be further provisions for dealing with contaminants contained in planning guidance or legislation made under the regime set out in Part IIA of the Environmental Protection Act 1990 which may be supplementary to the requirements of the Building Regulations. The Contaminated Land (England) Regulations 2000 make detailed provisions of a procedural nature to help give full effect to the Part IIA regime, and the statutory guidance provides a basis for enforcing authorities to apply the regime. Where contaminants are removed, treated or contained as part of the construction works, waste management law may apply. If waste is removed for off-site disposal, the 'Duty of Care' and/or special waste requirements[11] will apply.

0.10 Redevelopment is often the most effective means of remediating land affected by contaminants. This process is subject to controls under the Town and Country Planning Acts, and local planning authorities follow the guidance in PPG 23[12]. Although environmental protection, planning and Building Regulations have different purposes their aims are similar. Consequently the processes for assessing the effects of pollutants and contaminants are similar. An investigation or assessment to determine the characteristics of a site can be further developed for Building Regulations purposes when the form and construction of the buildings are known. If appropriate data are gathered at the early stages it should not be necessary to completely re-evaluate a site for Building Regulations purposes.

Authorities that should be notified about contamination

0.11 Other regulatory authorities may have an interest in land affected by contamination. It may be necessary at any stage of the site investigation, risk assessment or remediation process to notify any unexpected events or change in outcomes to these regulatory authorities. The most likely situations are:

- The Environmental Health department of the district council should be informed if contaminants are found on a site where the presence of contamination has not been formally recognised through the planning process, if it is found that contaminants from the site are affecting other land or if contaminants are reaching the site from neighbouring land. Additional discussions may also be required if the contamination identified differs from that which has been previously discussed and agreed with the local planning authority (LPA) or Environmental Health department.
- As redevelopment is the most favoured means of dealing with land affected by contaminants, all land quality issues should be set out in documents in support of planning approval sent to the local planning authority. As designs are refined it may be necessary to inform the LPA of any impacts the design changes may have on the risk assessment and remediation strategy.
- The Environment Agency has a number of relevant duties at sites where contamination may be an issue; in particular these include specific duties relating to waste management and the protection of water quality and resources. Sites may be of concern to the Environment Agency where there is a potential impact on controlled waters, if the site is designated as a Special Site under Part IIA of the Environmental Protection Act 1991, where an authorisation may be required or specific hazards are found. The local Environment Agency office should be contacted to identify if there are any relevant issues.
- Some remedial measures may themselves require prior authorisation from the Environment Agency including abstraction licensing for groundwater treatment and waste management licensing for a number of activities involving contaminated soils.

---

8 *Preparing for floods: interim guidance for improving the flood resistance of domestic and small business properties*, ODPM, 2002.

9 BRE for Scottish Office *Design guidance on flood damage for dwellings*, 1996.

10 CIRIA/Environment Agency Flood products. *Using flood protection products – a guide for home owners*, 2003. Available from: www.ciria.org/flooding.

11 Environmental Protection (Duty of Care (England)) Regulations 1991, as amended (SI 1991/2839 and SI 2003/63).

12 Planning Policy Guidance Note PPG 23 *Planning and pollution control*, DoE, 1997.

- Working on contaminated land can be hazardous. The risks should be assessed to meet the requirements of the Construction (Design and Management) Regulations 1994. Working procedures should be in accordance with the Construction (Health, Safety and Welfare) Regulations 1996. It may be necessary to give notice to the Health and Safety Executive prior to work starting.

Specific guidance on the assessment of land affected by contaminants is set out in Appendix A.

Definitions

0.12 The following meanings apply to terms throughout this Approved Document:

Building and land associated with the building.

The building and all the land forming the site subject to building operations which includes land under the building and the land around it which may have an effect on the building or its users (see also paragraph 2.11).

Contaminant. Any substance[13] which is or may become harmful to persons or buildings, including substances which are corrosive, explosive, flammable, radioactive or toxic.

Floor. Lower horizontal surface of any space in a building including finishes that are laid as part of the permanent construction.

Groundwater. Water in liquid form, either as a static water table or flowing through the ground.

Interstitial condensation. Deposition of liquid water from a vapour, occurring within or between the layers of the building envelope.

Moisture. Water in liquid, solid or gaseous form.

Precipitation. Moisture in any form falling from the atmosphere, usually as rain, sleet, snow or hail.

Roof. Any part of the external envelope of a building that is at an angle of less than 70° to the horizontal.

Spray. Water droplets driven by the wind from the surface of the sea or other bodies of water adjacent to buildings. Sea spray can be especially hazardous to materials because of its salt content.

Surface condensation. Deposition of liquid water from a vapour, occurring on visible surfaces within the building.

Vapour control layer. Material of construction, usually a membrane, that substantially reduces the water vapour transfer through any building in which it is incorporated.

Wall. Any opaque part of the external envelope of a building that is at an angle of 70° or more to the horizontal.

---

[13] Part IIA of the Environmental Protection Act 1990 defines substance as '...any natural or artificial substance, whether in solid or liquid form or in the form of gas or vapour.'

Section 1: Clearance or treatment of unsuitable material

SITE INVESTIGATION

1.1 The preparation of the site will depend on the findings of the site investigation. The site investigation is relevant to Sections 1, 2 and 3 of this Approved Document and also to the requirements of Approved Document A with respect to foundations. The site investigation should consist of a number of well-defined stages:

a. **Planning stage.** Clear objectives should be set for the investigation, including the scope and requirements, which enable the investigation to be planned and carried out efficiently and provide the required information;

b. **Desk study.** A review of the historical, geological and environmental information about the site is essential;

c. **Site reconnaissance or walkover survey.** This stage of the investigation facilitates the identification of actual and potential physical hazards and the design of the main investigation;

d. **Main investigation and reporting.** This will usually include intrusive and non-intrusive sampling and testing to provide soil parameters for design and construction. The main investigation should be preceded by (b) and (c) above.

1.2 The extent and level of investigation need to be tailored to the type of development and the previous use of land. Typically the site investigation should include susceptibility to groundwater levels and flow, underlying geology, and ground and hydro-geological properties. A geotechnical site investigation should identify physical hazards for site development, determine an appropriate design and provide soil parameters for design and construction. British Standard BS 5930:1999[14] provides comprehensive guidance on site investigations. Guidance on site investigation for low-rise buildings is given in six BRE Digests covering procurement[15], desk studies[16], the walk-over survey[17], trial pits[18], soil description[19] and direct investigation[20]. Reference should also be made to BS 8103-1:1995[21].

1.3 Where the site is potentially affected by contaminants, a combined geotechnical and geo-environmental investigation should be considered. Guidance on assessing and remediating sites affected by contaminants is given in Section 2: Resistance to contaminants.

UNSUITABLE MATERIAL

1.4 Vegetable matter such as turf and roots should be removed from the ground to be covered by the building at least to a depth to prevent later growth. The effects of roots close to the building also need to be assessed. Consideration should be given to whether this provision need apply to a building used wholly for:

a. storing goods, provided that any persons who are habitually employed in the building are engaged only in taking in, caring for or taking out the goods; or

b. a purpose such that the provision would not serve to increase protection to the health or safety of any persons habitually employed in the building.

1.5 Where mature trees are present on sites with shrinkable clays (see Diagram 1 and Table 1), the potential damage arising from ground heave to services and floor slabs and oversite concrete should be assessed. Reference should be made to BRE Digest 298[22]. Where soils and vegetation type would require significant quantities of soil to be removed, reference should be made to BRE Digests 240[23] and 241[24], and to the FBE (Foundation for the Built Environment) report[25]. The effects of remaining trees on services and building movements close to the building need to be assessed using guidance in NHBC (National House Building Council) Standards Chapter 4.2[26].

---

14 BS 5930:1999 Code of practice for site investigations.

15 BRE Digest 322 *Site investigation for low-rise building: procurement*, 1987.

16 BRE Digest 318 *Site investigation for low-rise building: desk studies*, 1987.

17 BRE Digest 348 *Site investigation for low-rise building: the walk-over survey*, 1989.

18 BRE Digest 381 *Site investigation for low-rise building: trial pits*, 1993.

19 BRE Digest 383 *Site investigation for low-rise building: soil description*, 1993.

20 BRE Digest 411 *Site investigation for low-rise building: direct investigations*, 1995.

21 BS 8103-1:1995 Structural design for low-rise buildings.

22 BRE Digest 298 *Low-rise building foundations: the influence of trees in clay soils*, 1999.

23 BRE Digest 240 *Low-rise buildings on shrinkable clay soils: Part 1*, 1993.

24 BRE Digest 241 *Low-rise buildings on shrinkable clay soils: Part 2*, 1993.

25 *Subsidence damage to domestic buildings: lessons learned and questions remaining*, FBE, 2000.

26 NHBC Standards Chapter 4.2 *Building near trees*, 2003.

Diagram 1 **Distribution of shrinkable clays and principal sulphate/sulphide bearing strata in England and Wales**

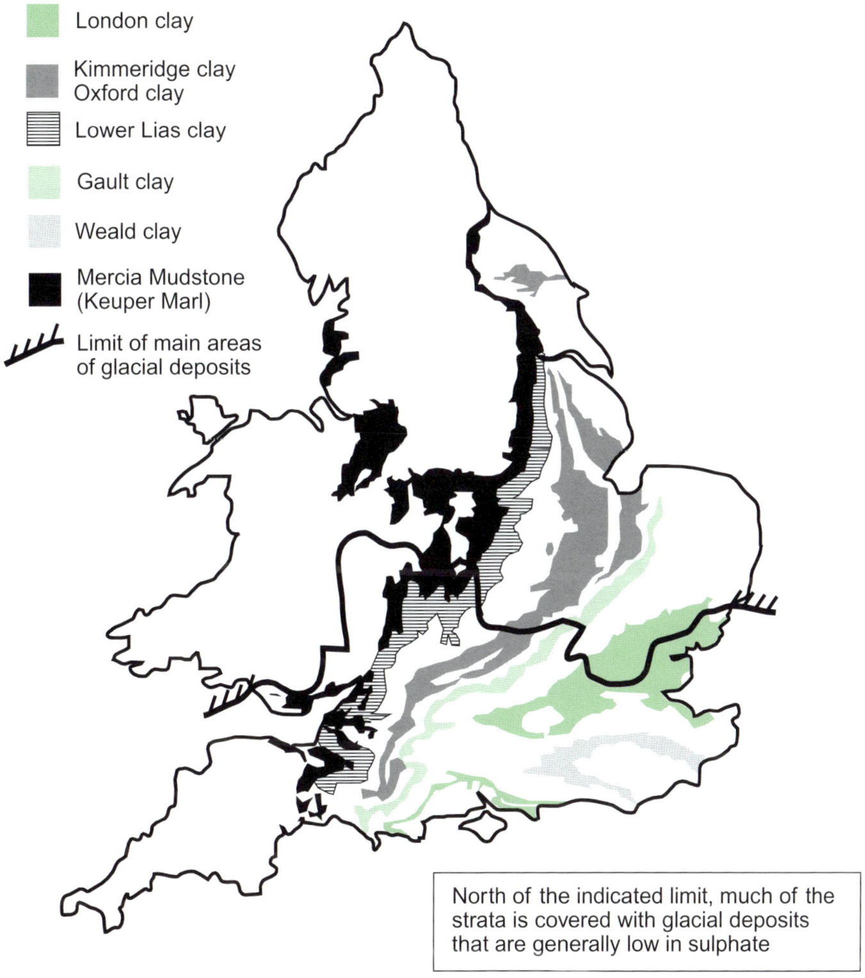

1.6 Building services such as below ground drainage should be sufficiently robust or flexible to accommodate the presence of any tree roots. Joints should be made so that roots will not penetrate them. Where roots could pose a hazard to building services, consideration should be given to their removal.

1.7 On sites previously used for buildings, consideration should be given to the presence of existing foundations, services, buried tanks and any other infrastructure that could endanger persons in and about the building and any land associated with the building.

1.8 Where the site contains fill or made ground, consideration should be given to its compressibility and its potential for collapse on wetting, and to appropriate remedial measures to prevent damaging differential settlement. Guidance is given in BRE Digest 427[27] and BRE Report BR 424[28].

Table 1 **Volume change potential for some common clays**

Clay type	Volume change potential
Glacial till	Low
London	High to very high
Oxford and Kimmeridge	High
Lower Lias	Medium
Gault	High to very high
Weald	High
Mercia Mudstone	Low to medium

27 BRE Digest 427 *Low-rise buildings on fill.*
28 BRE Report BR 424 *Building on fill: Geotechnical aspects, 2001.*

Section 2: Resistance to contaminants

INTRODUCTION

2.1 A wide range of solid, liquid and gaseous contaminants can arise on sites, especially those that have had a previous industrial use (see paragraph 0.12 for the definition of a contaminant). In particular, the burial of biodegradable waste in landfills can give rise to landfill gas (see paragraph 2.25). Sites with a generally rural use such as agriculture or forestry may be contaminated by pesticides, fertiliser, fuel and oils and decaying matter of biological origin.

2.2 Table 2 lists examples of sites that are likely to contain contaminants. It is derived from the 'Industry Profile' guides produced by the former Department of the Environment (DoE), each of which deals with a different industry with the potential to cause contamination[29]. Each profile identifies contaminants which may be associated with the industry, areas on the site in which they may be found and possible routes for migration. The Department for the Environment, Food and Rural Affairs (Defra)/Environment Agency publication CLR 8[30] presents a selection of contaminants that may be relevant for the assessment of land affected by contaminants as they are likely to be found on a large number of industrial sites across the UK.

2.3 In addition, there can be problems of natural contaminants in certain parts of the country as a result of the underlying geology. In this instance the contaminants can be naturally occurring heavy metals (e.g. cadmium and arsenic) originating in mining areas, and gases (e.g. methane and carbon dioxide) originating in coal mining areas and from organic rich soils and sediments such as peat and river silts. The Environment Agency has produced two guidance documents[31,32] on this subject which discuss the geographical extent of these contaminants, the associated hazards, methods of site investigation and protective measures.

2.4 Natural contaminants also include the radioactive gas radon, although the specific approach for assessing and managing the risks it poses is different from other contaminants (see paragraphs 2.39 to 2.41).

2.5 Sulphate attack affecting concrete floor slabs and oversite concrete associated with particular strata also needs to be considered. Principal areas of sulphate bearing strata in England and Wales are shown in Diagram 1 and Table 1. BRE Special Digest SD1[33] provides guidance on investigation, concrete specification and design to mitigate the effects of sulphate attack.

Table 2 **Examples of sites likely to contain contaminants**
Animal and animal products processing works
Asbestos works
Ceramics, cement and asphalt manufacturing works
Chemical works
Dockyards and dockland
Engineering works (including aircraft manufacturing, railway engineering works, shipyards, electrical and electronic equipment manufacturing works)
Gas works, coal carbonisation plants and ancillary by-product works
Industries making or using wood preservatives
Landfill and other waste disposal sites
Metal mines, smelters, foundries, steel works and metal finishing works
Munitions production and testing sites
Oil storage and distribution sites
Paper and printing works
Power stations
Railway land, especially larger sidings and depots
Road vehicle fuelling, service and repair: garages and filling stations
Scrap yards
Sewage works, sewage farms and sludge disposal sites
Tanneries
Textile works and dye works
Note: the above list is not exhaustive

29 Department of the Environment Industry Profiles, 1996.
30 Defra/Environment Agency Contaminated Land Research Report CLR 8 *Priority contaminants for the assessment of land*, 2002.
31 Environment Agency R & D Technical Report P291 *Information on land quality in England: Sources of information (including background contaminants).*
32 Environment Agency R & D Technical Report P292 *Information on land quality in Wales: Sources of information (including background contaminants).*
33 BRE Special Digest SD1 *Concrete in aggressive ground*, 2003

Diagram 2 **Example of a conceptual model for a site showing source–pathway–receptor**

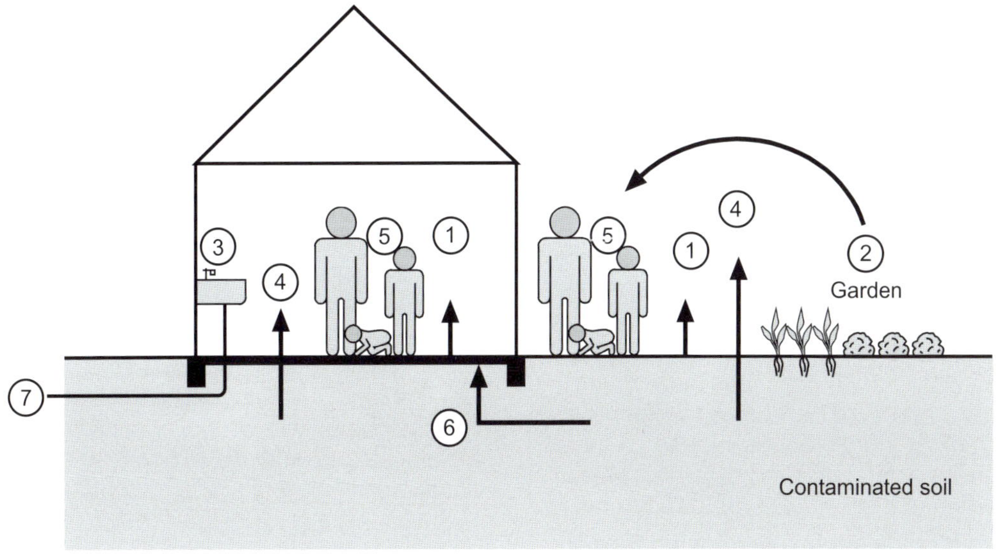

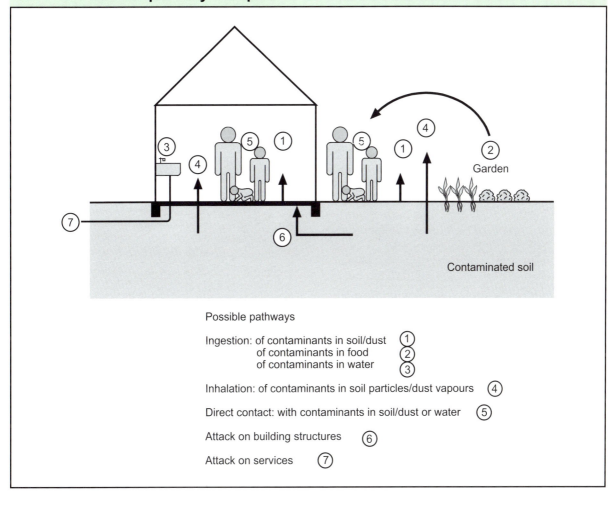

Possible pathways

Ingestion: of contaminants in soil/dust ①
of contaminants in food ②
of contaminants in water ③

Inhalation: of contaminants in soil particles/dust vapours ④

Direct contact: with contaminants in soil/dust or water ⑤

Attack on building structures ⑥

Attack on services ⑦

SOLID AND LIQUID CONTAMINANTS

Risk assessment

General concepts

2.6 To ensure safe development of land affected by contaminants the principles of risk assessment (as set out in paragraph 2.8 below) should be followed. The general approach is founded on the concept of the 'source–pathway–receptor' relationship, or pollutant linkage, where source refers to contaminants in or on the ground. This is illustrated by the conceptual model[34] in Diagram 2.

2.7 When land affected by contaminants is developed, receptors (i.e. buildings, building materials and building services, as well as people) are introduced onto the site and so it is necessary to break the pollutant linkages. This can be achieved by:

a. treating the contaminant (e.g. use of physical, chemical or biological processes to eliminate or reduce the contaminant's toxicity or harmful properties);

b. blocking or removing the pathway (e.g. isolating the contaminant beneath protective layers or installing barriers to prevent migration);

c. protecting or removing the receptor (e.g. changing the form or layout of the development, using appropriately designed building materials, etc.);

d. removing the contaminant (e.g. excavating contaminated material).

[34] The conceptual model is a textual or schematic hypothesis of the nature and sources of contamination, the pollution migration pathways and potential receptors, developed on the basis of the information from a preliminary assessment, and is refined during subsequent phases of investigation.

Stages of risk assessment

2.8 In assessing the risks for land contamination a tiered approach is adopted with an increasing level of detail required in progressing through the tiers. The three tiers are: preliminary risk assessment, generic quantitative risk assessment (GQRA) and detailed quantitative risk assessment (DQRA). Once the need for a risk assessment has been identified, it will always be necessary to undertake a preliminary risk assessment but, depending on the situation and the outcome, it may not be appropriate to do a more detailed risk assessment. Alternatively, it may be necessary to do only one or both of the more detailed risk assessments. For each tier, the model procedures for the management of land contamination (CLR 11, *Consultation draft 2003*) describes the stages of risk assessment that should be followed for identifying risks and making judgements about the consequences of land affected by contamination when developing a site. These are outlined below:

a. **Hazard identification – developing the conceptual model by establishing contaminant sources, pathways and receptors.** This is the preliminary site assessment which consists of a desk study and a site walk-over in order to obtain sufficient information to obtain an initial understanding of the potential risks. An initial conceptual model for the site can be based on this information.

b. **Hazard assessment – identifying what pollutant linkages may be present and analysing the potential for unacceptable risks.** Collect further information and undertake exploratory site investigation to refine understanding of risks and the likelihood of pollutant linkages. The results may be interpreted using generic criteria and assumptions.

c. **Risk estimation – establishing the scale of the possible consequences by considering the degree of harm that may result and to which receptors.** Undertake detailed ground investigation to collect sufficient data to estimate the risks the contaminants may pose to defined receptors under defined conditions of exposure.

d. **Risk evaluation – deciding whether the risks are acceptable or unacceptable.** Review all site data to decide whether estimated risks are unacceptable, taking into account the nature and scale of any uncertainties associated with the risk estimation process.

2.9 Guidance on the investigation of sites potentially affected by contaminants is provided in:

a. the Association of Geotechnical and Geoenvironmental Specialists (AGS) document[35];

b. BS 5930:1999[36];

c. BS 10175:2001[37]; and

d. the Environment Agency documents[38-45].

They recommend a risk based approach to identify and quantify the hazards that may be present and the nature of the risk they may pose. They describe the design and execution of field investigations, including suitable sample distribution strategies, sampling and testing.

Hazard identification and assessment

2.10 A preliminary site assessment is required to provide information on the past and present uses of the site and surrounding area that may give rise to contamination (see Table 2). During the site walk-over there may be signs of possible contaminants (see Table 3). The information collated from the desk study and site walk-over can assist and will dictate the design of the exploratory and detailed ground investigation.

---

35 Guidelines for combined geoenvironmental and geotechnical investigations, Association of Geotechnical and Geoenvironmental Specialists.

36 BS 5930:1999 Code of practice for site investigations.

37 BS 10175:2001 Investigation of potentially contaminated sites. Code of practice.

38 National Groundwater & Contaminated Land Centre report NC/99/38/2 *Guide to good practice for the development of conceptual models and the selection and application of mathematical models of contaminant transport processes in the subsurface.*

39 Defra/Environment Agency Contaminated Land Research Report CLR 7 *Assessment of risks to human health from land contamination: an overview of the development of soil guideline values and related research*, 2002.

40 Defra/Environment Agency Contaminated Land Research Report CLR 8 *Priority contaminants for the assessment of land*, 2002.

41 Defra/Environment Agency Contaminated Land Research Report CLR 9 *Contaminants in soil: collation of toxicological data and intake values for humans*, 2002.

42 Defra/Environment Agency Contaminated Land Research Report CLR 10 *The contaminated land exposure assessment model (CLEA): technical basis and algorithms*, 2002.

43 Defra/Environment Agency Contaminated Land Research Report CLR 11 *Handbook of model procedures for the management of contaminated land (in preparation).*

44 Environment Agency R & D Technical Report P5-065 *Technical aspects of site investigation*, 2000.

45 Environment Agency R & D Technical Report P5-066 *Secondary model procedure for the development of appropriate soil sampling strategies for land contamination.*

2.11 The site assessment and risk evaluation should pay particular attention to the area of the site subject to building operations. Those parts of the land associated with the building that include the building itself, gardens and other places on the site that are accessible to users of the building and those in and about the building should be remediated to the requirements of the Building Regulations.

There may be a case for a lower level of remediation if part of, or the remainder of, the land associated with the building, or adjacent to such land, is accessible to a lesser extent to the user or those in and about the building than the main parts of the buildings and their respective gardens. This incremental approach may also apply when very large sites are subject to redevelopment in stages; it may be possible to limit remediation to the site that is subject to building operations.

In all cases the risk evaluation and remediation strategy documentation is likely to be appropriate for demonstrating that restricted remediation is acceptable. The onus is on the applicant to show why part of a site may be excluded from particular remediation measures.

Even if the adjacent land is not subject to Building Regulations, which are concerned with health and safety, it may still be subject to planning control legislation or to control under Part IIA of the Environmental Protection Act 1990.

2.12 The Planning Authority should be informed prior to any intrusive investigations or if any substance is found which is at variance with any preliminary statements made about the nature of the site.

Risk estimation and evaluation

2.13 The detailed ground investigation must provide sufficient information for the confirmation of a conceptual model for the site, the risk assessment and the design and specification of any remedial works. This is likely to involve collection and analysis of soil, soil gas, surface and groundwater samples by the use of invasive and/or non-invasive techniques. An investigation of the groundwater regime, levels and flows is essential for most sites since elevated groundwater levels could bring contaminants close to the surface both beneath the building and in any land associated with the building. Expert advice should be sought but further guidance and information are provided in Annex A.

2.14 During the development of land affected by contaminants the health and safety of both the public and workers should be considered[46,47].

Table 3 **Examples of possible contaminants**

Signs of possible contaminants	Possible contaminant
Vegetation (absence, poor or unnatural growth)	Metals Metal compounds
	Organic compounds Gases (landfill or natural source)
Surface materials (unusal colours and contours may indicate wastes and residues)	Metals Metal compounds
	Oily and tarry wastes
	Asbestos
	Other mineral fibres
	Organic compounds including phenols
	Combustible material including coal and coke dust
	Refuse and waste
Fumes and odours (may indicate organic chemicals)	Volatile organic and/or sulphurous compounds from landfill or petrol/ solvent spillage
	Corrosive liquids
	Faecal animal and vegetable matter (biologically active)
Damage to exposed foundations of existing buildings	Sulphates
Drums and containers (empty or full)	Various

Note: the above list is not exhaustive

Remedial measures

Introduction

2.15 If unacceptable risks to the defined receptor have been identified then these need to be managed through appropriate remedial measures. The risk management objectives are defined by the need to break the pollutant linkages using the methods outlined in paragraph 2.6 and described below. Other objectives will also need to be considered such as timescale, cost, remedial works, planning constraints and sustainability. Depending on the contaminant, three generic types of remedial measures can be considered: treatment, containment and removal. The containment or treatment of waste may require a waste management licence from the Environment Agency.

46 HSE Report HSG 66 *Protection of workers and the general public during the development of contaminated land*, 1991.

47 CIRIA Report 132 *A guide to safe working practices for contaminated land*, 1993.

When building work is undertaken on sites affected by contaminants where control measures are already in place, care must be taken not to compromise these measures. For example, cover systems may be breached when new building foundations are constructed, such as when extensions are added.

Treatment

2.16 A wide range of treatment processes is now available for dealing with contaminants. Biological, chemical and physical techniques carried out either in or ex situ exist which may decrease one or more of the following features of the contaminants: mass, concentration, mobility, flux or toxicity. The choice of the most appropriate technique for a particular site is a highly site-specific decision for which specialist advice should be sought.

Containment

2.17 Containment in its widest sense usually means encapsulation of material containing contaminants but in the context of building development containment is often taken to mean cover systems. However, in-ground vertical barriers may also be required to control lateral migration of contaminants.

2.18 Cover systems involve the placement of one or more layers of materials over the site to achieve one or more of the following objectives:

a. break the pollutant linkage between receptors and contaminants;

b. sustain vegetation;

c. improve geotechnical properties; and

d. reduce exposure to an acceptable level.

2.19 Some of the building structures, e.g. foundations, sub-structure and ground floor, may, dependent on the circumstances and construction, contribute to measures to provide effective protection of health from contaminants.

2.20 Imported fill and soil for cover systems should be assessed at source to ensure that it is not contaminated above specified concentrations and meets required standards for vegetation[48]. Design and dimensioning of cover systems, particularly soil based ones typically used for gardens, should take account of their long-term performance where intermixing of the soil cover with the contaminants in the ground can take place. Maintenance and monitoring may be necessary. Gradual intermixing due to natural effects and activities such as burrowing animals, gardening, etc. needs to be considered. Excavations by householders for garden features, etc. can penetrate the cover layer and may lead to exposure to contaminants. Further guidance on the design, construction and performance of cover layers is given in the Construction Industry Research and Information Association (CIRIA) Report SP124[49].

Removal

2.21 This involves the excavation and safe disposal to licensed landfill of the contaminants and contaminated material. Excavation can be targeted to contaminant 'hot spots', or it may be necessary to remove sufficient depth of contaminated material to accommodate a cover system within the planned site levels. Removal may not be viable depending on the extent and depth of the contaminants on the site and the availability of suitably licensed landfills. Imported fill should be assessed at source to ensure that there are no materials that will pose unacceptable risks to potential receptors.

2.22 Further detailed guidance on all three types of remedial measure is given in the Environment Agency/NHBC R & D Publication 66 referred to above and in a series of CIRIA publications[50–55].

Risks to buildings, building materials and services

2.23 The hazards to buildings, building materials and services on sites affected by contaminants need to be considered since these are also receptors. The hazards to consider are:

a. **Aggressive substances.** These include inorganic and organic acids, alkalis, organic solvents and inorganic chemicals such as sulphates and chlorides which may affect the long-term durability of construction materials (such as concrete, metals and plastics).

b. **Combustible fill.** This includes domestic waste, colliery spoil, coal, plastics, petrolsoaked ground, etc. which, if ignited, may lead to subterranean fires and consequent damage to the structural stability of buildings, and the integrity or performance of services.

c. **Expansive slags.** The two main types are blast furnace and steel making slag which may expand some time after deposition – usually when water is introduced onto the site – causing damage to buildings and services.

---

48 BS 3882:1994 Specification for topsoil.

49 CIRIA Special Publication SP124 *Barriers, liners and cover systems for containment and control of land contamination*, 1996.

50 CIRIA Special Publication SP102 *Decommissioning, decontamination and demolition*, 1995.

51 CIRIA Special Publication SP104 *Classification and selection of remedial methods*, 1995.

52 CIRIA Special Publication SP105 *Excavation and disposal*, 1995.

53 CIRIA Special Publication SP106 *Containment and hydraulic measures*, 1996.

54 CIRIA Special Publication SP107 *Ex-situ remedial methods for soils, sludges and sediments*, 1995.

55 CIRIA Special Publication SP109 *In-situ methods of remediation*, 1995.

d. **Floodwater affected by contaminants.** Substances in the ground, waste matter or sewage may contaminate floodwater. This contaminated water may affect building elements, such as walls or ground floors, that are close to or in the ground. Guidance on resistant construction can be found in *Preparing for floods*[56] *or Design guidance on flood damage to dwellings*[57].

2.24 Although the building and building materials are the main receptors with these hazards, ultimately there could be harm to health. A particular concern is the effect of hydrocarbons permeating potable water pipes made of polyethylene. Guidance on reducing these risks is given in a Water Research Centre report[58]. Further guidance on the assessment and management of risks to building materials is given in an Environment Agency document[59].

METHANE AND OTHER GASES FROM THE GROUND

Introduction

2.25 The term 'methane and other gases' is used to define hazardous soil gases which either originate from waste deposited in landfill sites or are generated naturally. It does not include radon which is dealt with separately in paragraphs 2.39 to 2.41. However, the term does include volatile organic compounds (VOCs). As stated in Limitations on Requirements above, measures described in this document are the minimum that are needed to comply with the Building Regulations. Further actions may be necessary to deal with the requirements of other legislation.

2.26 Landfill gas is generated by the action of micro-organisms on biodegradable waste materials in landfill sites. It generally consists of methane and carbon dioxide together with small quantities of VOCs which give the gas its characteristic odour. Methane and oxygen deficient atmospheres (sometimes referred to as stythe or black-damp) containing elevated levels of carbon dioxide and nitrogen can be generated naturally in coal mining areas. Methane and carbon dioxide can also be produced by organic rich soils and sediments such as peat and river silts. A wide range of VOCs can also be present as a result of petrol, oil and solvent spillages. Methane and other gases can migrate through the subsoil and through cracks and fissures into buildings.

2.27 Methane is an explosive and asphyxiating gas. Carbon dioxide although non-flammable is toxic. VOCs are not only flammable and toxic but can also have a strong, unpleasant odour. Should any of these gases build up to hazardous levels in buildings then they can cause harm to health or compromise safety.

Risk assessment

2.28 The risk assessment process outlined in paragraph 2.8 should also be adopted for methane and other gases. Further investigation for hazardous soil gases may be required where the ground to be covered by the building and/or any land associated with the building is:

a. On a landfill site, within 250m of the boundary of a landfill site or where there is suspicion that it is within the sphere of influence of such a site. The Environment Agency's policy on building development on or near to landfills should be followed.

b. On a site subject to the wide scale deposition of biodegradable substances (including made ground or fill).

c. On a site that has been subject to a use that could give rise to petrol, oil or solvent spillages.

d. In an area subject to naturally occurring methane, carbon dioxide and other hazardous gases (e.g. hydrogen sulphide).

2.29 There are documents that cover hazardous soil gases in these specific contexts:

a. Waste Management Paper No. 27[60] gives guidance on the generation and movement of landfill gas as well as techniques for its investigation. Complementary guidance is given in a document 61 by the Chartered Institution of Wastes Management (CIWM).

---

56 *Preparing for floods: interim guidance for improving the flood resistance of domestic and small business properties*, ODPM, 2002.

57 BRE for Scottish Office *Design guidance on flood damage for dwellings*, TSO, 1996.

58 Foundation for Water Research Report FR0448 *Laying potable water pipelines in contaminated ground: guidance notes*, 1994.

59 *Assessment and management of risks to buildings, building materials and services from land contamination*, Environment Agency, 2001.

60 HMIP Waste Management Paper No. 27 *Landfill gas*, 2nd edition, 1991.

61 *Monitoring of landfill gas*, Chartered Institution of Wastes Management (CIWM), 2nd edition, 1998.

b. The Institute of Petroleum has prepared a guidance document covering petroleum retail sites[62].

c. The BGS report on naturally occurring methane and other gases[63] gives guidance on the geographical extent of these contaminants, the associated hazards and methods of site investigation. This is supported by a report sponsored by the former DoE on methane and other gases in disused coal mining areas[64].

d. In addition, CIRIA has produced three relevant guidance documents on methane and other gases which describe how such gases are generated and move within the ground[65], methods of detection and monitoring[66] and investigation strategies[67].

2.30 During a site investigation for methane and other gases it is important to take measurements over a sufficiently long period of time in order to characterise gas emissions fully. This should also include periods when gas emissions are likely to be higher, e.g. during periods of falling atmospheric pressure. It is also important to establish not only the concentration of these gases in the ground but also the quantity of gas generating materials, their rate of gas generation, gas movement in the ground and gas emissions from the ground surface. This is an important part of the risk estimation stage. Indications about the gas regime in the ground can be obtained through surface emission rate and borehole flow rate measurements, and guidance on this is given in CIRIA Reports 151[68] and 152[69].

2.31 Construction activities undertaken as part of building development can alter the gas regime on the site. For example, a site strip can increase surface gas emissions as can piling and excavation for foundations, and dynamic compaction can push dry biodegradable waste into moist, gas-active zones.

2.32 There are no Soil Guideline Values (see Annex A) for methane and other gases. When assessing gas risks in the context of traditional housing there is a need to consider two pathways for human receptors: (i) gas entering the dwelling through the sub-structure, and building up to hazardous levels, and (ii) subsequent householder exposure in garden areas which can include where outbuildings (e.g. garden sheds and greenhouses) and extensions are constructed, and where there may also be excavations for garden features (e.g. ponds).

2.33 Guidance on undertaking gas risk assessment is given in CIRIA Report 152[69], and the GaSIM model is also available for assessing gas emissions from landfill sites[70]. There is further discussion of gas risk assessment in the forthcoming Defra/Environment Agency document CLR 11[71].

2.34 CIRIA Report 149[72] and the Department of the Environment, Transport and the Regions (DETR) Partners in Technology (PIT) report[73] describe a range of ground gas regimes (defined in terms of soil gas concentrations of methane and carbon dioxide as well as borehole flow rate measurements) which can be helpful in assessing gas risks.

2.35 Depending on the proposed use, for non-domestic development the focus might be on the building only, but the general approach is the same.

Remedial measures

2.36 If the risks posed by the gas are unacceptable then these need to be managed through appropriate building remedial measures. Site-wide gas control measures may be required if the risks on any land associated with the building are deemed unacceptable. Such control measures include removal of the gas generating material or covering together with gas extraction systems. Further guidance is contained in CIRIA Report 149[72]. Generally speaking, expert advice should be sought in these circumstances.

2.37 Gas control measures for dwellings consist of a gas resistant barrier across the whole footprint (i.e. walls and floor) above an extraction (or ventilation) layer from which gases can be dispersed and vented to the atmosphere. They are normally passive, i.e. gas flow is driven by stack (temperature difference) and wind effects. Consideration should be given to the design and layout of buildings to maximise the driving forces of natural ventilation. Further guidance on this and detailed practical guidance on the construction of protective measures for housing is given in the BRE/Environment Agency report

---

62 Institute of Petroleum TP 95 *Guidelines for investigation and remediation of petroleum retail sites*, 1998.

63 BGS Technical Report WP/95/1 *Methane, carbon dioxide and oil seeps from natural sources and mining areas: characteristics, extent and relevance to planning and development in Great Britain*, 1995.

64 *Methane and other gases from disused coal mines: the planning response*, DoE, 1996.

65 CIRIA Report 130 *Methane: its occurrence and hazards in construction*, 1993.

66 CIRIA Report 131 *The measurement of methane and other gases from the ground*, 1993.

67 CIRIA Report 150 *Methane investigation strategies*, 1995.

68 CIRIA Report 151 *Interpreting measurements of gas in the ground*, 1995.

69 CIRIA Report 152 *Risk assessment for methane and other gases from the ground*, 1995.

70 Environment Agency GasSIM – Landfill gas assessment tool.

71 Defra/Environment Agency Contaminated Land Research Report CLR 11 *Handbook of model procedures for the management of land contamination*, 2004.

72 CIRIA Report 149 *Protecting development from methane*, 1995.

BR 414[73]. (In order to accommodate gas resistant membrane, for example as shown in BR414, the position and type of insulation may have to be adjusted). The DETR/Arup Environmental report[74] compares the performance of a range of commonly used gas control measures and can be used as a guide to the design of such measures.

2.38 Gas control measures for non-domestic buildings use the same principles as those used for housing, and the DETR/Arup Environmental report can also be used as a guide to design. Expert advice should be sought as the floor area of such buildings can be large and it is important to ensure that gas is adequately dispersed from beneath the floor. The use of mechanical (as opposed to passive) systems and monitoring and alarm systems may be necessary. There is a need for continued maintenance and calibration of these systems, so they are more appropriate with non-domestic buildings (as opposed to dwellings) since there is usually scope for this. Again, expert advice should be sought. Special sub-floor ventilation systems are carefully designed to ensure adequate performance and should not be modified unless subjected to a specialist review of the design. Such ventilation systems, particularly those using powered ventilation, are unlikely to be appropriate for owner occupied properties as there is a risk of interference by users.

RADON

2.39 Radon is a naturally occurring radioactive colourless and odourless gas which is formed in small quantities by radioactive decay wherever uranium and radium are found. It can move through the subsoil and so into buildings. Some parts of the country, notably the West Country, have higher levels than elsewhere. Exposure to high levels for long periods increases the risk of developing lung cancer. To reduce this risk all new buildings, extensions and conversions, whether residential or non-domestic, built in areas where there may be elevated radon emissions, may need to incorporate precautions against radon.

2.40 Guidance on the areas susceptible to radon and practical protective measures has been published by the BRE as Report BR 211[75]. This guidance was developed to show radon protective measures for dwellings.

A European Council Directive establishes a common basis for radiation protection legislation in all Member States. The Ionising Radiations Regulations[76] set a national reference level for radon gas and employers and self-employed persons responsible for a workplace are required to measure radon levels on being directed to do so. See also the HSE/BRE guide 'Radon in the workplace'[77].

There is at present no guidance on protection from radon in the workplace but some of the techniques used for installing a radon resistant membrane, described in BR 211, may be suitable for use in domestic sized buildings with heating and ventilation regimes similar to those used in dwellings. The guidance in BR 211 can be used as the basis for radon protection of other building types but this should be done with caution. Information in 'Radon in the workplace' provides guidance for existing non-domestic buildings.

Interim guidance on extensions can be found in GBG 25 Buildings and radon[78].

2.41 Although the precise areas where measures should be taken are listed in the BRE Report, these are reviewed by ODPM (Office of the Deputy Prime Minister) in the light of advice from the National Radiological Protection Board (NRPB) and the British Geological Survey (BGS). Current information on the areas delineated by ODPM for the purposes of Building Regulations should be obtained from local authority building control officers or from approved inspectors. Changes to areas delineated as requiring radon protection will be notified to building control bodies and will be posted on the ODPM website.

---

73 BRE/Environment Agency Report BR 414 *Protective measures for housing on gas-contaminated land*, 2001.
74 DETR/Arup Environmental PIT Research Report: *Passive venting of soil gases beneath buildings*, 1997.
75 BRE Report BR 211 *Radon: guidance on protective measures for new dwellings*, 1999.
76 The Ionising Radiations Regulations 1999 (SI 1999/3232).
77 BRE Report BR 293 *Radon in the workplace*, 1995.
78 BRE GBG 25 *Buildings and radon*, 1996.

Section 3: Subsoil drainage

3.1 The provisions which follow assume that the site of the building is not subject to general flooding (see paragraph 0.8) or, if it is, that appropriate steps are being taken.

3.2 Where the water table can rise to within 0.25m of the lowest floor of the building, or where surface water could enter or adversely affect the building, either the ground to be covered by the building should be drained by gravity, or other effective means of safeguarding the building should be taken.

3.3 If an active subsoil drain is cut during excavation and if it passes under the building it should be:

a. re-laid in pipes with sealed joints and have access points outside the building; or

b. re-routed around the building; or

c. re-run to another outfall (see Diagram 3).

3.4 Where there is a risk that groundwater beneath or around the building could adversely affect the stability and properties of the ground, consideration should be given to site drainage or other protection (see Section 4: Floors).

3.5 For protecting low lying buildings or basements from localised flooding where foul water drainage also receives rainwater, refer to Approved Document H (Drainage and waste disposal). In heavy rainfall these systems surcharge and where preventative measures are not taken this could lead to increased risks of flooding within the property.

3.6 Flooding can create blockages in drains and sewers that can lead to backflow of sewage into properties through low level drain gullies, toilets, etc. Guidance on anti-flooding devices is given in a CIRIA publication[79].

3.7 General excavation work for foundations and services can alter groundwater flows through the site. Where contaminants are present in the ground, consideration should be given to subsoil drainage to prevent the transportation of water-borne contaminants to the foundations or into the building or its services.

---

[79] CIRIA Publication C506 *Low-cost options for prevention of flooding from sewers*, 1998.

Diagram 3 **Subsoil drain cut during excavation**

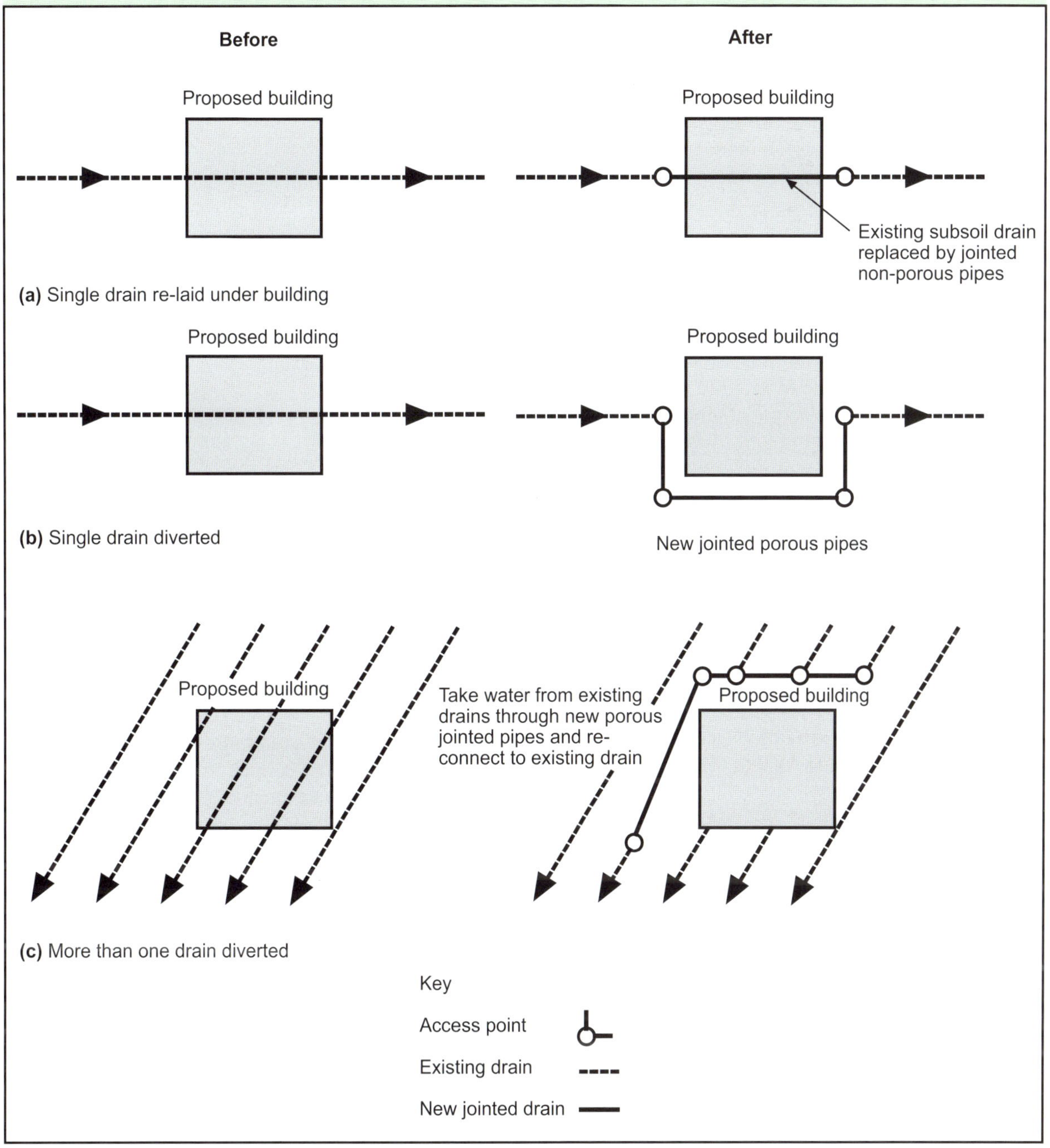
Before
After
Proposed building
Proposed building
Existing subsoil drain replaced by jointed non-porous pipes
(a) Single drain re-laid under building
Proposed building
Proposed building
(b) Single drain diverted
New jointed porous pipes
Proposed building
Take water from existing drains through new porous jointed pipes and re-connect to existing drain
Proposed building
(c) More than one drain diverted
Key
Access point
Existing drain
New jointed drain

Section 4: Floors

4.1 This section gives guidance for five situations:

a. ground supported floors exposed to moisture from the ground (see paragraphs 4.6 to 4.12);

b. suspended timber ground floors exposed to moisture from the ground (see paragraphs 4.13 to 4.16);

c. suspended concrete ground floors exposed to moisture from the ground (see paragraphs 4.17 to 4.20);

d. the risk of interstitial condensation in ground floors and floors exposed from below (see paragraph 4.21);

e. the risk of surface condensation and mould growth on any type of floor (see paragraph 4.22).

4.2 Floors next to the ground should:

a. resist the passage of ground moisture to the upper surface of the floor;

b. not be damaged by moisture from the ground;

c. not be damaged by groundwater;

d. resist the passage of ground gases. To meet requirement C1 (2) floors in some localities may need to resist the passage of hazardous ground gases such as radon or methane. Remedial measures will include a gas resistant barrier which, with proper detailing, can also function as a damp proof membrane. For specific guidance for methane and other gases refer to paragraphs 2.25 to 2.38, and for radon refer to paragraphs 2.39 to 2.41. Guidance is provided in reports BR 414[80] and BR 211[81] respectively.

4.3 Consideration should be given to whether 4.2(a) need apply to a building used wholly for:

a. storing goods, provided that any persons who are habitually employed in the building are engaged only in taking in, caring for or taking out the goods; or

b. a purpose such that the provision would not serve to increase protection to the health or safety of any persons habitually employed in the building.

4.4 Floors next to the ground and floors exposed from below should be designed and constructed so that their structural and thermal performance are not adversely affected by interstitial condensation.

4.5 All floors should not promote surface condensation or mould growth, given reasonable occupancy conditions.

GROUND SUPPORTED FLOORS (MOISTURE FROM THE GROUND)

4.6 Any ground supported floor will meet the requirement if the ground is covered with dense concrete laid on a hardcore bed and a damp-proof membrane is provided. Suitable insulation may be incorporated.

Technical solution

4.7 Unless it is subjected to water pressure, which is likely in the case of buildings on very permeable strata such as chalk, limestone or gravel (in which case see Alternative approach, paragraph 4.12), a concrete ground supported floor may be built as follows (Diagram 4):

a. well compacted hardcore bed, no greater than 600mm deep[82], of clean, broken brick or similar inert material, free from materials including water-soluble sulphates in quantities which could damage the concrete (BRE Digest 276[83]; and

b. concrete at least 100mm thick (but thicker if the structural design requires) to mix ST2 in BS 8500 or, if there is embedded reinforcement, to mix ST4 in BS 8500[84]; and

c. damp-proof membrane above or below the concrete, and continuous with the damp-proof courses in walls, piers and the like. If the ground could contain water soluble sulphates, or there is any risk that sulphate or other deleterious matter could contaminate the hardcore, the membrane should be placed at the base of the concrete slab[85].

---

80 BRE/Environment Agency Report BR 414 *Protective measures for housing on gas-contaminated land*, 2001.

81 BRE Report BR 211 *Radon: guidance on protective measures for new dwellings*, 1999.

82 If the hardcore bed is deeper than 600mm, there may be a risk of excessive settlement and cracking of the floor slab. In such cases, a suspended floor slab is advised.

83 BRE Digest 276 *Hardcore*, 1992.

84 BS 8500-1:2002 Concrete. Complementary British Standard to BS EN 206-1 Method of specifying and guidance for the specifier.

85 BRE Special Digest SD1 *Concrete in aggressive ground*, 2003.

Diagram 4 **Ground supported floor – construction (see paragraph 4.7)**

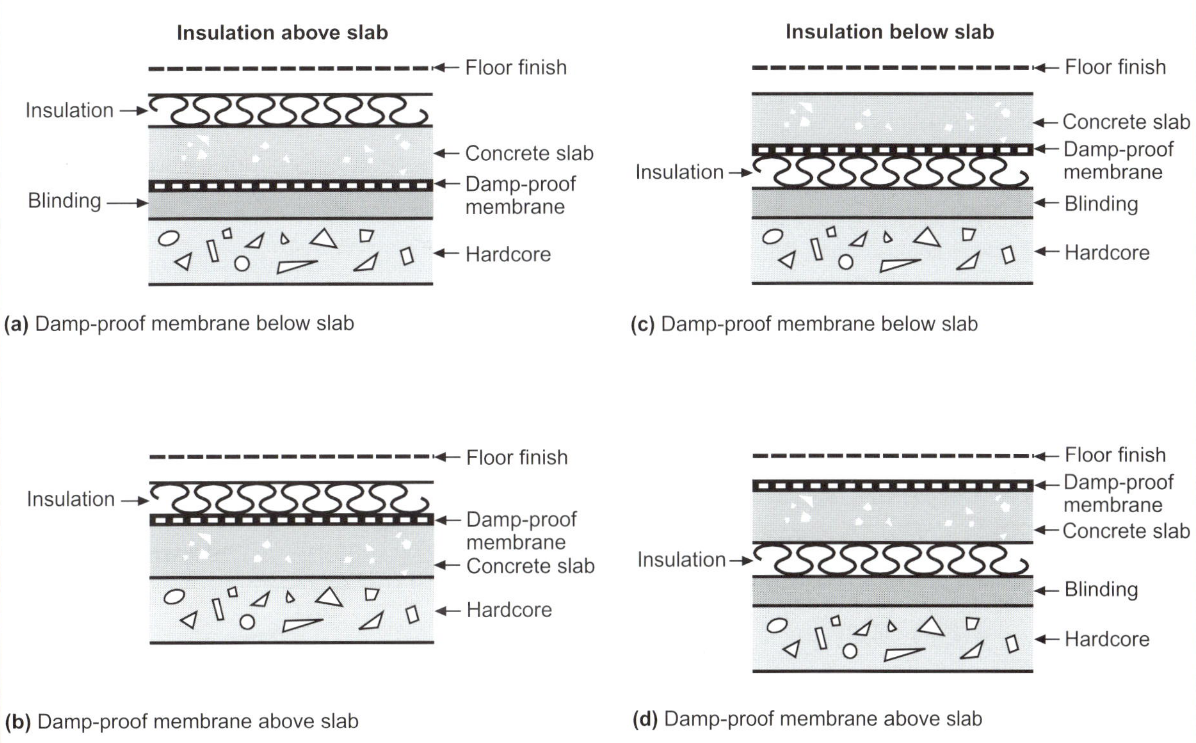

4.8 A membrane below the concrete could be formed with a sheet of polyethylene, which should be at least 300μm thick (1200 gauge) with sealed joints and laid on a bed of material that will not damage the sheet.

4.9 A membrane laid above the concrete may be either polyethylene sheet as described above (but without the bedding material) or three coats of cold applied bitumen solution or similar moisture and water vapour resisting material. In each case it should be protected by either a screed or a floor finish, unless the membrane is pitchmastic or similar material which will also serve as a floor finish.

4.10 Insulants placed beneath floor slabs should have sufficient strength to resist the weight of the slab and the anticipated floor loading as well as any possible overloading during construction. In order to resist degradation insulation that is placed below the damp-proof membrane should have low water absorption. If necessary the insulant should be resistant to contaminants in the ground.

4.11 A timber floor finish laid directly on concrete may be bedded in a material which may also serve as a damp-proof membrane. Timber fillets laid in the concrete as a fixing for a floor finish should be treated with an effective preservative unless they are above the damp-proof membrane. Some preservative treatments are described in BS 1282:1999[86].

Alternative approach

4.12 The requirement can also be achieved by following the relevant recommendations of Clause 11 of BS CP 102:1973[87]. BS 8102:1990[88] includes recommendations for floors subject to water pressure.

SUSPENDED TIMBER GROUND FLOORS (MOISTURE FROM THE GROUND)

4.13 Any suspended timber floor next to the ground will meet the requirement if:

a. the ground is covered so as to resist moisture and prevent plant growth; and

b. there is a ventilated air space between the ground covering and the timber; and

c. there are damp-proof courses between the timber and any material which can carry moisture from the ground.

86 BS 1282:1999 Wood preservatives. Guidance on choice, use and application.

87 BS CP 102:1973 Protection of buildings against water from the ground.

88 BS 8102:1990 Code of practice for protection of structures against water from the ground.

Technical solution

4.14 Unless it is covered with a floor finish which is highly vapour resistant (in which case see the Alternative approach in paragraph 4.16), a suspended timber floor next to the ground may be built as follows (Diagram 5):

a. Ground covering either:

   i. unreinforced concrete at least 100mm thick to mix ST 1 in BS 8500[89]. The concrete should be laid on a compacted hardcore bed of clean, broken brick or any other inert material free from materials including water-soluble sulphates in quantities which could damage the concrete; or

   ii. concrete, composed as described above, or inert fine aggregate, in either case at least 50mm thick laid on at least 300μm (1200 gauge) polyethylene sheet with sealed joints, and itself laid on a bed of material which will not damage the sheet.

   To prevent water collecting on the ground covering, either the top should be entirely above the highest level of the adjoining ground or, on sloping sites, consideration should be given to installing drainage on the outside of the up-slope side of the building (see Diagram 6).

b. Ventilated air space measuring at least 75mm from the ground covering to the underside of any wall -plates and at least 150mm to the underside of the suspended timber floor (or insulation if provided). Two opposing external walls should have ventilation openings placed so that the ventilating air will have a free path between opposite sides and to all parts. The openings should be not less than either 1,500mm^2/m run of external wall or 500mm^2/m^2 of floor area, whichever gives the greater

Diagram 5 **Suspended timber floor – construction (see paragraph 4.14(a) (i))**

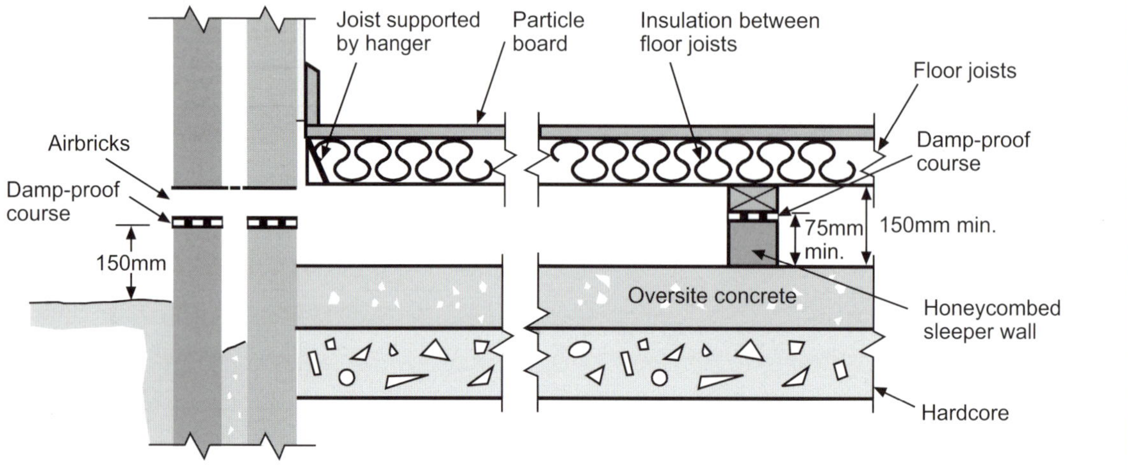

Diagram 6 **Suspended floor – preventing water collection (see paragraph 4.14(a))**

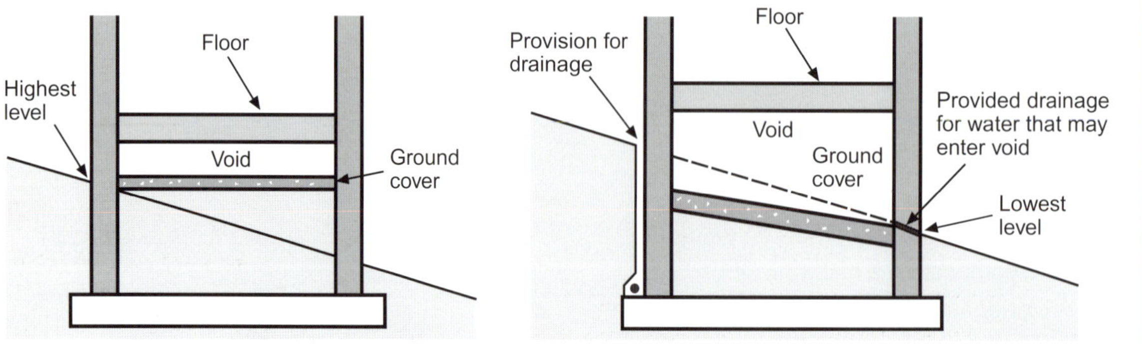

Note: Slope has been exaggerated for clarity

89 BS 8500-1:2002 Concrete. Complementary British Standard to BS EN 206-1 Method of specifying and guidance for the specifier.

opening area. Any pipes needed to carry ventilating air should have a diameter of at least 100mm. Ventilation openings should incorporate suitable grilles which prevent the entry of vermin to the sub-floor but do not resist the air flow unduly. If floor levels need to be nearer to the ground to provide level access sub-floor ventilation can be provided through offset (periscope) ventilators.

c. Damp-proof courses of impervious sheet material, engineering brick or slates in cement mortar or other material which will prevent the passage of moisture. Guidance for choice of materials is given in BS 5628:Part 3:2001[90].

d. In shrinkable clay soils, the depth of the air space may need to be increased to allow for heave.

4.15 In areas such as kitchens, utility rooms and bathrooms where water may be spilled, any board used as a flooring, irrespective of the storey, should be moisture resistant. In the case of chipboard it should be of one of the grades with improved moisture resistance specified in BS 7331:1990[91] or BS EN 312 Part 5:1997[92]. It should be laid, fixed and jointed in the manner recommended by the manufacturer. To demonstrate compliance the identification marks should be facing upwards. Any softwood boarding should be at least 20mm thick and from a durable species[93] or treated with a suitable preservative.

Alternative approach

4.16 The requirement can also be met (see paragraph 4.14 above) by following the relevant recommendations of Clause 11 of BS CP 102:1973[94].

SUSPENDED CONCRETE GROUND FLOORS (MOISTURE FROM THE GROUND)

4.17 Any suspended floor of in situ or precast concrete, including beam and block floors, next to the ground will meet the requirement if it will adequately prevent the passage of moisture to the upper surface and if the reinforcement is protected against moisture.

Technical solution

4.18 One solution for a suspended concrete floor could be:

a. in situ concrete at least 100mm thick (but thicker if the structural design requires) containing at least 300kg of cement for each m^3 of concrete; or

b. precast concrete construction with or without infilling slabs; and

c. reinforcing steel protected by concrete cover of at least 40mm if the concrete is in situ and at least the thickness required for a moderate exposure if the concrete is precast.

4.19 A suspended concrete floor will meet the requirements if it incorporates:

a. a damp-proof membrane (if the ground below the floor has been excavated below the lowest level of the surrounding ground and will not be effectively drained); and

b. a ventilated air space. This should measure at least 150mm clear from the ground to the underside of the floor (or insulation if provided). Two opposing external walls should have ventilation openings placed so that the ventilating air will have a free path between opposite sides and to all parts of the floor void. The openings should be not less than either $1500mm^2/m$ run of external wall or $500mm^2/m^2$ of floor area, whichever gives the greater opening area. Any pipes needed to carry ventilating air should have a diameter of at least 100mm. Ventilation openings should incorporate suitable grilles which prevent the entry of vermin to the sub-floor but do not resist the air flow unduly.

4.20 In localities where flooding is likely, consideration may be given to including means of inspecting and clearing out the sub-floor voids beneath suspended floors. For guidance, see the DTLR publication on preparing for floods[95].

---

90 BS 5628-3:2001 Code of practice for use of masonry. Materials and components, design and workmanship.

91 BS 7331:1990 Specification for direct surfaced wood chipboard based on thermosetting resins.

92 BS EN 312-5:1997 Particleboards. Specifications. Requirements for load-bearing boards for use in humid conditions.

93 BRE Digest 429 Timbers and their natural durability and resistance to preservative treatment, 1998.

94 BS CP 102:1973 Protection of buildings against water from the ground.

95 *Preparing for floods: interim guidance for improving the flood resistance of domestic and small business properties*, ODPM, 2002.

Diagram 7 **Typical floors exposed from below**

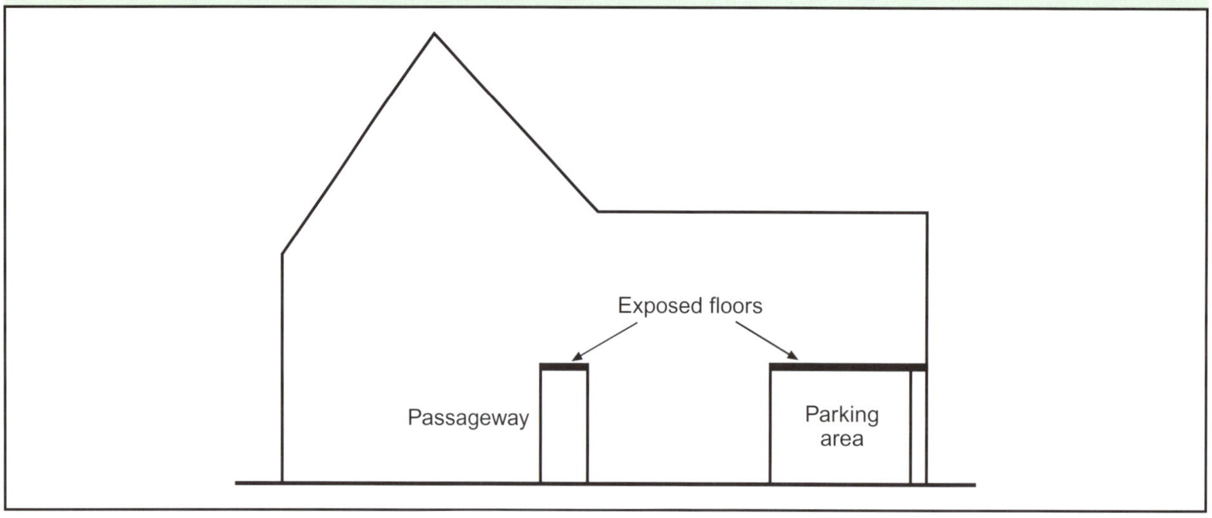

GROUND FLOORS AND FLOORS EXPOSED FROM BELOW (RESISTANCE TO DAMAGE FROM INTERSTITIAL CONDENSATION)

4.21 A ground floor or floor exposed from below, i.e. above an open parking space or passageway, as shown in Diagram 7, will meet the requirement if it is designed and constructed in accordance with Clause 8.5 and Appendix D of BS 5250:2002[96], BS EN ISO 13788:2002[97] and BR 262[98].

FLOORS (RESISTANCE TO SURFACE CONDENSATION AND MOULD GROWTH)

4.22 A floor will meet the requirement if:

a. a ground floor is designed and constructed so that the thermal transmittance (U-value) does not exceed $0.7 W/m^2K$ at any point; and

b. in the case of all floors, the junctions between elements are designed in accordance with the recommendations in the report[99] on robust construction details, or follow the guidance of BRE IP17/01[100].

---

96 BS 5250:2002 Code of practice for the control of condensation in buildings.

97 BS EN ISO 13788:2002 Hygrothermal performance of building components and building elements. Internal surface temperature to avoid critical surface humidity and interstitial condensation. Calculation methods.

98 BRE Report BR 262 *Thermal insulation: avoiding risks*, 2002.

99 *Limiting thermal bridging and air leakage: robust construction details for dwellings and similar buildings*, DTLR, 2001.

100 BRE Information Paper IP17/01 *Assessing the effects of thermal bridging at junctions and around openings*, 2001.

Section 5: Walls

5.1 This section gives guidance for four situations:

a. internal and external walls exposed to moisture from the ground (see paragraphs 5.4 to 5.6);

b. external walls exposed to precipitation from the outside, covering:

   i. solid external walls (see paragraphs 5.8 to 5.11);

   ii. cavity external walls (see paragraphs 5.12 to 5.15);

   iii. framed external walls (see paragraph 5.17);

   iv. cracking of walls (see paragraph 5.18);

   v. impervious cladding systems (see paragraphs 5.19 to 5.28);

   vi. the joint between window and door frames and external walls and door thresholds (see paragraphs 5.29 to 5.33);

c. the risk of interstitial condensation in any type of wall (see paragraphs 5.34 to 5.35);

d. the risk of surface condensation or mould growth on any type of wall (see paragraph 5.36).

A wall includes piers, columns and parapets. It also includes chimneys if they are attached to the building. It does not include windows, doors and similar openings, but does include the joint between their frames and the wall. In the following, the term 'precipitation' includes the effects of spray blown from the sea or any other body of water adjacent to the building.

5.2 Walls should:

a. resist the passage of moisture from the ground to the inside of the building; and

b. not be damaged by moisture from the ground and not carry moisture from the ground to any part which would be damaged by it, and, if the wall is an external wall:

c. resist the penetration of precipitation to components of the structure that might be damaged by moisture; and

d. resist the penetration of precipitation to the inside of the building; and

e. be designed and constructed so that their structural and thermal performance are not adversely affected by interstitial condensation; and

f. not promote surface condensation or mould growth, given reasonable occupancy conditions.

5.3 Consideration should be given to whether provisions 5.2(a) and (d) need apply to a building used wholly for:

a. storing goods, provided that any persons who are habitually employed in the building are engaged only in taking in, caring for or taking out the goods; or

b. a purpose such that the provision would not serve to increase protection to the health or safety of any persons habitually employed in the building.

INTERNAL AND EXTERNAL WALLS (MOISTURE FROM THE GROUND)

5.4 Any internal or external wall will meet the requirement if a damp proof course is provided.

Technical solution

5.5 An internal or external wall will meet the requirement if it is built as follows (unless it is subject to groundwater pressure, in which case see the Alternative approach – paragraph 5.6):

a. damp-proof course of bituminous material, polyethylene, engineering bricks or slates in cement mortar or any other material that will prevent the passage of moisture. The damp proof course should be continuous with any damp-proof membrane in the floors; and

b. if the wall is an external wall, the damp-proof course should be at least 150mm above the level of the adjoining ground (see Diagram 8), unless the design is such that a part of the building will protect the wall; and

c. if the wall is an external cavity wall (see Diagram 9a) the cavity should be taken down at least 225mm below the level of the lowest damp-proof course, or a damp-proof tray should be provided so as to prevent precipitation passing into the inner leaf (see Diagram 9b), with weep holes every 900mm to assist in the transfer of moisture through the external leaf. Where the damp-proof tray does not extend the full length of the exposed wall, i.e. above an opening, stop ends and at least two weep holes should be provided.

Alternative approach

5.6 The requirement can also be met by following the relevant recommendations of Clauses 4 and 5 of BS 8215:1991[101]. BS 8102:1990[102]

---

101 BS 8215:1991 Code of practice for design and installation of damp-proof courses in masonry construction.

102 BS 8102:1990 Code of practice for protection of structures against water from the ground.

Diagram 8 **Damp-proof courses (see paragraph 5.5(b))**

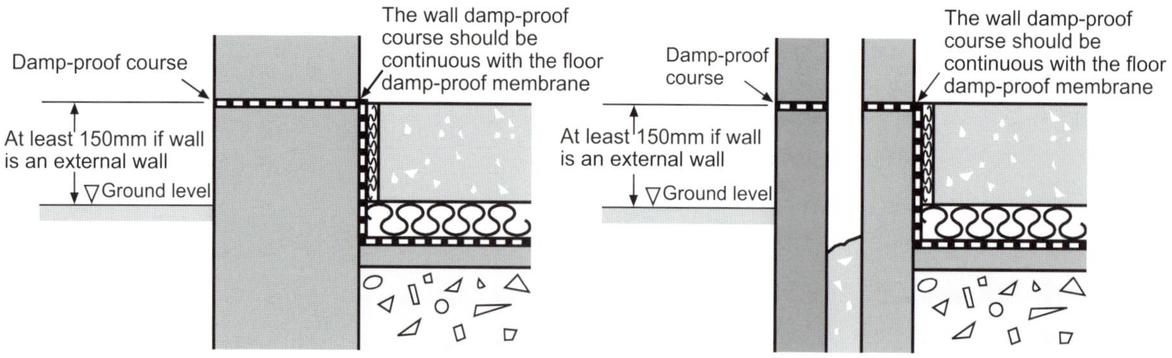

Diagram 9 **Protecting inner leaf (see paragraph 5.5(c))**

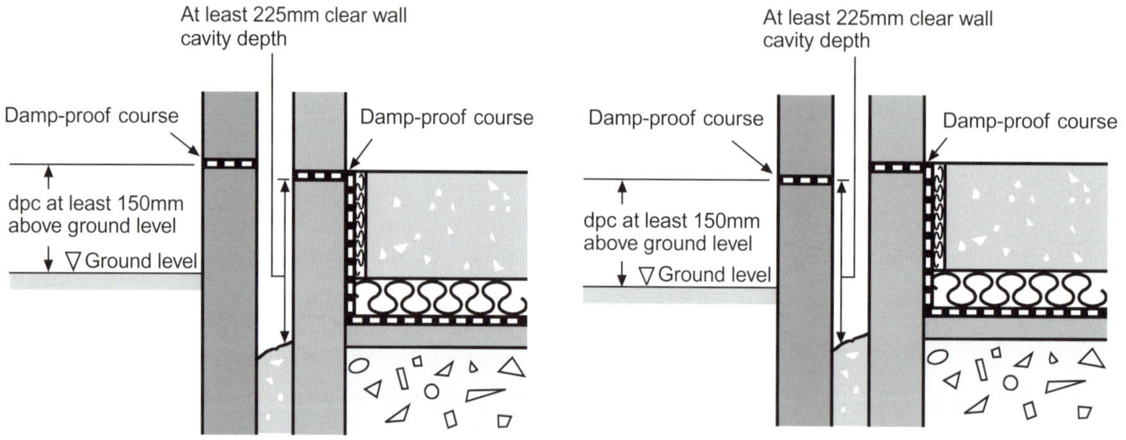

(a) Cavity carried down

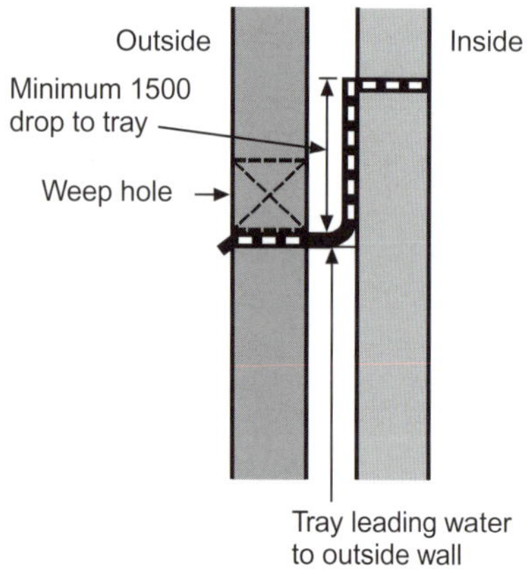

(b) Damp proof (cavity) tray

includes recommendations for walls subject to groundwater pressure including basement walls.

EXTERNAL WALLS (MOISTURE FROM THE OUTSIDE)

5.7 As well as giving protection against moisture from the ground, an external wall should give protection against precipitation. This protection can be given by a solid wall of sufficient thickness (see paragraphs 5.8 to 5.11), or by a cavity wall (see paragraphs 5.12 to 5.18), or by an impervious or weather-resisting cladding (see paragraphs 5.19 to 5.28).

SOLID EXTERNAL WALLS

5.8 Any solid wall will meet the requirement if it will hold moisture arising from rain and snow until it can be released in a dry period without penetrating to the inside of the building, or causing damage to the building. The wall thickness will depend on the type of brick and block and on the severity of wind-driven rain. A method of describing the exposure to wind-driven rain is given in BS 8104:1992[103]; see also BS 5628-3:2001[104].

Technical solution

5.9 A solid external wall in conditions of **very severe** exposure should be protected by external impervious cladding, but in conditions of **severe** exposure may be built as follows:

a. **brickwork or stonework** at least 328mm thick, dense aggregate concrete **blockwork** at least 250mm thick, or lightweight aggregate or aerated autoclaved concrete **blockwork** at least 215mm thick; and

b. **rendering**: the exposed face of the bricks or blocks should be rendered or be given no less protection. Rendering should be in two coats with a total thickness of at least 20mm and should have a scraped or textured finish. The strength of the mortar should be compatible with the strength of the bricks or blocks. The joints, if the wall is to be rendered, should be raked out to a depth of at least 10mm. Further guidance is given in BS EN 998:2003[105]. The rendering mix should be one part of cement, one part of lime and six parts of well graded sharp sand (nominal mix 1:1:6) unless the blocks are of dense concrete aggregate, in which case the mix may be 1:0.5:4. BS 5262:1991[106] includes recommendations for a wider range of mixes according to the severity of exposure and the type of brick or block.

   Premixed and proprietary renders should be used in accordance with the manufacturer's instructions;

Diagram 10 **Protection of wall head from precipitation (see paragraph 5.9(c))**

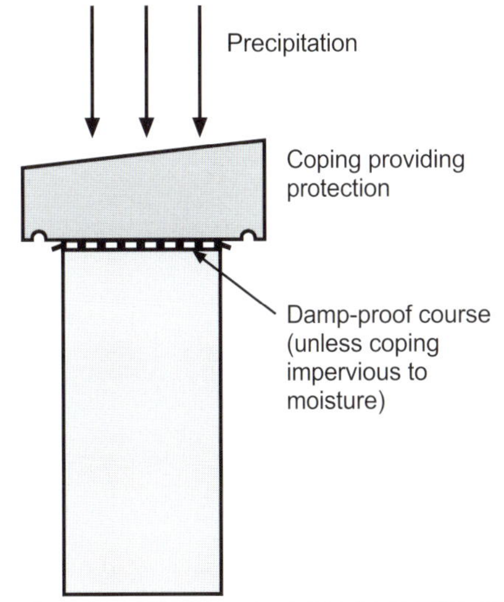

c. **protection** should be provided where the top of walls, etc. would otherwise be unprotected (see Diagram 10). Unless the protection and joints will be a complete barrier to moisture, a damp-proof course should also be provided;

d. **damp-proof courses, cavity trays and closers** should be provided and designed to ensure that water drains outwards:

   i. where the downward flow will be interrupted by an obstruction, such as some types of lintel; and

   ii. under openings, unless there is a sill and the sill and its joints will form a complete barrier; and

   iii. at abutments between walls and roofs.

5.10 Insulation. A solid external wall may be insulated on the inside or on the outside. Where it is on the inside a cavity should be provided to give a break in the path for moisture and where it is on the outside it should provide some resistance to the ingress of moisture to ensure the wall remains relatively dry (see Diagram 11).

---

103 BS 8104:1992 Code of practice for assessing exposure of walls to wind-driven rain.

104 BS 5628-3:2001 Code of practice for use of masonry. Materials and components, design and workmanship.

105 BS EN 998-2:2003 Specification for mortar for masonry. Masonry mortar.

106 BS 5262:1991 Code of practice for external renderings.

Alternative approach

5.11 The requirement can also be met by following the relevant recommendations of BS 5628-3:2001[107]. The code describes alternative constructions to suit the severity of the exposure and the type of brick or block.

CAVITY EXTERNAL WALLS

5.12 Any external cavity wall will meet the requirement if the outer leaf is separated from the inner leaf by a drained air space, or in any other way which will prevent precipitation from being carried to the inner leaf.

Technical solution

5.13 The construction of a cavity external wall could include:

a. outer leaf masonry (bricks, blocks, stone or manufactured stone); and

b. cavity at least 50mm wide. The cavity is to be bridged only by wall ties, cavity trays provided to prevent moisture being carried to the inner leaf (see paragraph 5.15 for cavity insulation), and cavity barriers, firestops and cavity closures, where appropriate; and

c. inner leaf masonry or frame with lining.

Masonry units should be laid on a full bed of mortar with the cross joints substantially and continuously filled to ensure structural robustness and weather resistance.

Where a cavity is to be partially filled, the residual cavity should not be less than 50mm wide (see Diagram 11).

Alternative approach

5.14 The requirement can also be met by following the relevant recommendations of BS 5628-3:2001[108]. The code describes factors affecting rain penetration of cavity walls.

CAVITY INSULATION

5.15 A full or partial fill insulating material may be placed in the cavity between the outer leaf and an inner leaf of masonry subject to the following conditions:

a. The suitability of a wall for installing insulation into the cavity should be determined either by reference to the map in Diagram 12 and the associated Table 4 or following the calculation or assessment procedure in current British or CEN standards. When partial fill materials are to be used, the residual cavity should not be less than 50mm nominal; and

b. A rigid (board or batt) thermal insulating material built into the wall should be the subject of current certification from an appropriate body or a European Technical Approval and the work should be carried out in accordance with the requirements of that document; or

c. Other insulating materials inserted into the cavity after the wall has been constructed should have certification from an appropriate body and be installed in accordance with the appropriate installations code. The suitability of the wall for filling is to be assessed before the work is carried out and the person undertaking the work should operate under an Approved Installer Scheme that includes an assessment of capability. Alternatively the insulating material should be the subject of current certification from an appropriate body or a European Technical Approval and the work should be carried out in accordance with the requirements of that document by operatives either directly employed by the holder of the document or employed by an installer approved to operate under the document; or

d. Urea-formaldehyde foam inserted into the cavity should be in accordance with BS 5617:1985[109] and be installed in accordance with BS 5618:1985[110]. The suitability of the wall for foam filling is to be assessed before the work is carried out and the person undertaking the work should operate under an Approved Installer Scheme that includes an assessment of capability.

e. When the cavity of an existing house is being filled, special attention should be given to the condition of the external leaf of the wall, e.g. its state of repair and type of pointing. Guidance is given in BS 8208-1:1985[111]. Some materials that are used to fill existing cavity walls may have a low risk of moisture being carried over to the internal leaf of the wall. In cases where a third party assessment of such a cavity fill material contains a method of assessing the construction of the walls and exposure risk, the procedure set out below may be replaced by that method.

---

107 BS 5628-3:2001 Code of practice for use of masonry. Materials and components, design and workmanship.

108 BS 5628-3:2001 Code of practice for use of masonry. Materials and components, design and workmanship.

109 BS 5617:1985 Specification for urea-formaldehyde (UF) foam systems suitable for thermal insulation of cavity walls with masonry or concrete inner and outer leaves.

110 BS 5618:1985 Code of practice for thermal insulation of cavity walls (with masonry or concrete inner and outer leaves) by filling with urea-formaldehyde (UF) foam systems.

111 BS 8208-1:1985 Guide to assessment of suitability of external cavity walls for filling with thermal insulation.

Diagram 11 **Insulated external walls: examples (see paragraphs 5.10 and 5.13)**

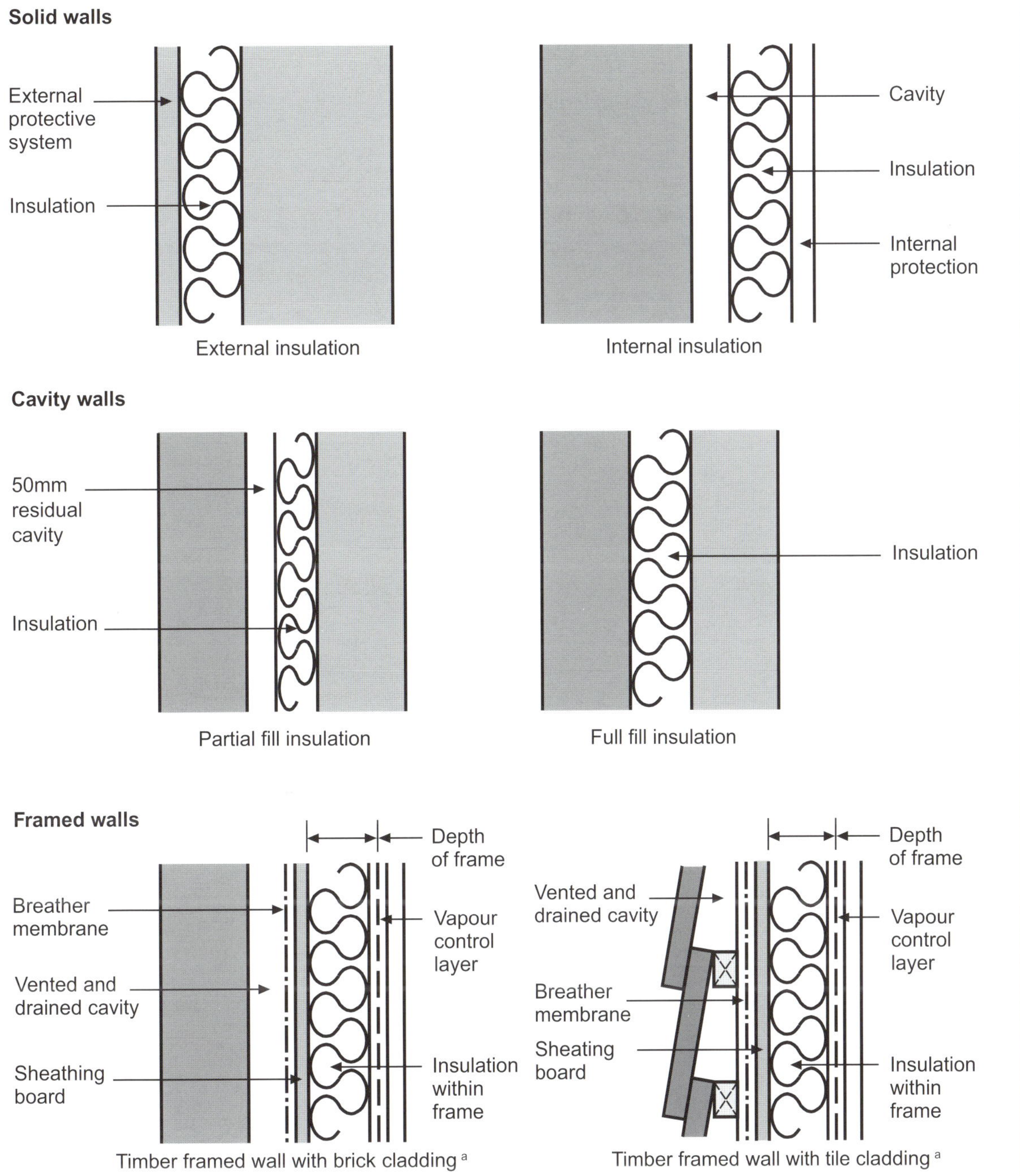

Note: a) In the case of light steel frame the insulation inside the cavity is placed over the frame.

Diagram 12 UK zones for exposure to driving rain

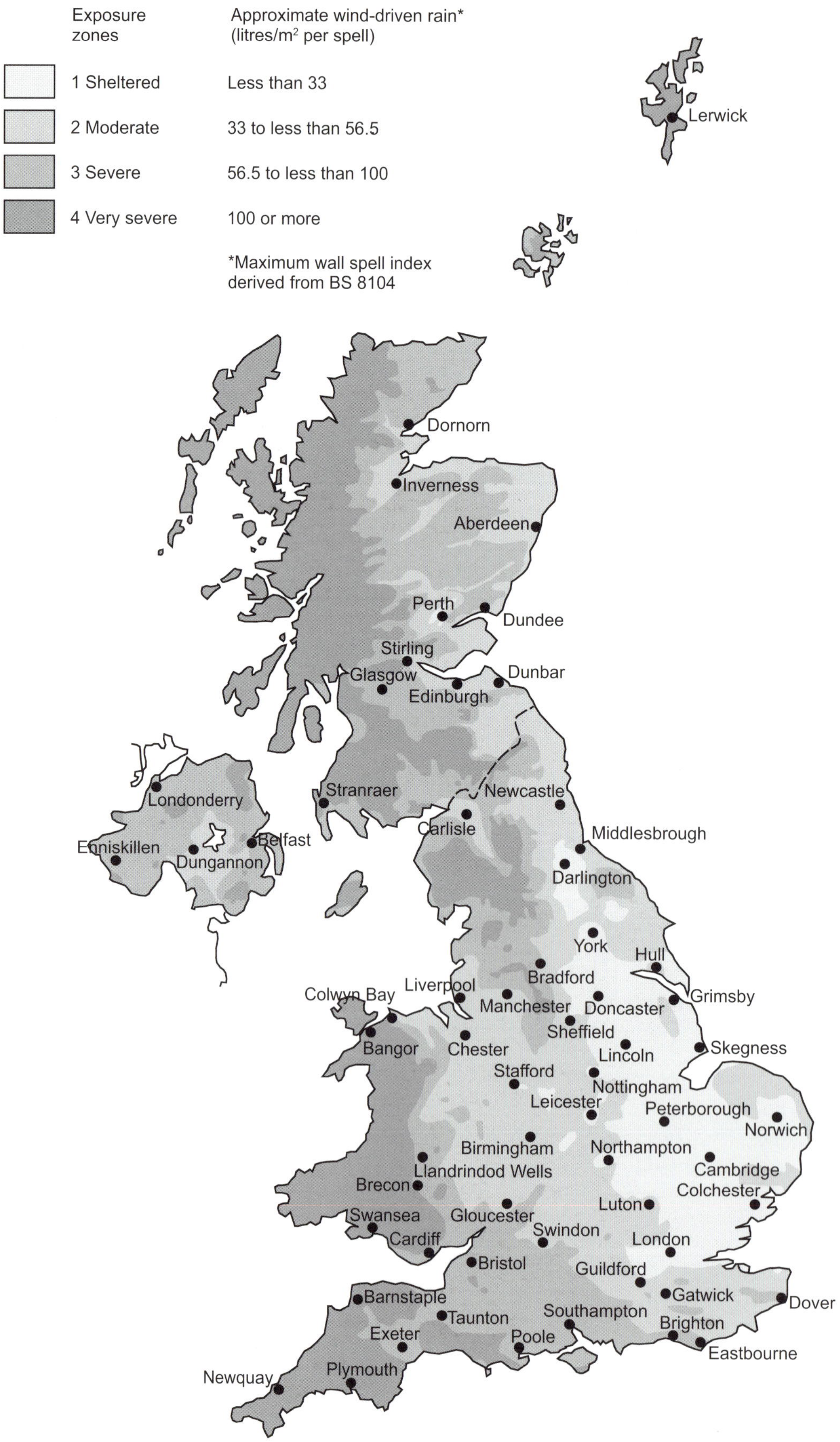
Exposure zones
Approximate wind-driven rain* (litres/m² per spell)
1 Sheltered
Less than 33
2 Moderate
33 to less than 56.5
3 Severe
56.5 to less than 100
4 Very severe
100 or more
*Maximum wall spell index derived from BS 8104
Lerwick
Dornorn
Inverness
Aberdeen
Perth
Dundee
Stirling
Glasgow
Edinburgh
Dunbar
Stranraer
Newcastle
Carlisle
Middlesbrough
Darlington
Londonderry
Enniskillen
Dungannon
Belfast
York
Hull
Bradford
Grimsby
Colwyn Bay
Liverpool
Manchester
Doncaster
Sheffield
Bangor
Chester
Lincoln
Skegness
Stafford
Nottingham
Leicester
Peterborough
Norwich
Birmingham
Northampton
Llandrindod Wells
Cambridge
Brecon
Colchester
Luton
Swansea
Gloucester
Swindon
Cardiff
London
Bristol
Guildford
Barnstaple
Gatwick
Dover
Taunton
Southampton
Brighton
Exeter
Poole
Eastbourne
Newquay
Plymouth

Table 4 **Maximum recommended exposure zones for insulated masonry walls**

Wall construction		Maximum recommended exposure zone for each construction						
Insulation method	**Min. width of filled or clear cavity (mm)**	**Impervious cladding**		**Rendered finish**		**Facing masonry**		
		Full height of wall	Above facing masonry	Full height of wall	Above facing masonry	Tooled flush joints	Recessed mortar joints	Flush sills and copings
Built-in full fill	50	4	3	3	3	2	1	1
	75	4	3	4	3	3	1	1
	100	4	4	4	3	3	1	2
	125	4	4	4	3	3	1	2
	150	4	4	4	4	4	1	2
Injected fill not UF foam	50	4	2	3	2	2	1	1
	75	4	3	4	3	3	1	1
	100	4	3	4	3	3	1	1
	125	4	4	4	3	3	1	2
	150	4	4	4	4	4	1	2
Injected fill UF foam	50	4	2	3	2	1	1	1
	75	4	2	3	2	2	1	1
	100	4	2	3	2	2	1	1
Partial fill								
Residual 50mm cavity	50	4	4	4	4	3	1	1
Residual 75mm cavity	75	4	4	4	4	4	1	1
Residual 100mm cavity	100	4	4	4	4	4	2	1
Internal insulation								
Clear cavity 50mm	50	4	3	4	3	3	1	1
Clear cavity 100mm	100	4	4	4	4	4	2	2
Fully filled cavity 50mm	50	4	3	3	3	2	1	1
Fully filled cavity 100mm	100	4	4	4	3	3	1	2

5.16 If the map given in Diagram 12 is used, determine the national exposure and, where appropriate, apply the following modifiers:

i. where local conditions accentuate wind effects, such as open hillsides or valleys where the wind is funnelled onto the wall, add one to this exposure zone value;

ii. where walls do not face into the prevailing wind, subtract one from this exposure zone value.

(The national exposure zone value can be more accurately calculated from the larger scale maps and correction factors given in BS 8104:1992[112].)

112 BS 8104:1992 Code of practice for assessing exposure of walls to wind-driven rain.

Determine the recommended constructions from the modified exposure zone values given in Table 4. Further guidance as to the use of this table is given in BRE Report 262[113].

FRAMED EXTERNAL WALLS

5.17 Any framed external wall will meet the requirement if the cladding is separated from the insulation or sheathing by a vented and drained cavity with a membrane that is vapour open, but resists the passage of liquid water, on the inside of the cavity (see Diagram 11).

CRACKING OF EXTERNAL WALLS

5.18 Severe rain penetration may occur through cracks in masonry external walls caused by thermal movement in hot weather or subsidence after prolonged droughts. The possibility of this should be taken into account when designing a building. Detailed guidance is given in:

a. BRE Building Elements: Walls, windows and doors[114]; and

b. BRE Report 292[115];

c. Guidance for choice of materials is given in BS5628-3:2001[116].

IMPERVIOUS CLADDING SYSTEMS FOR WALLS

5.19 Cladding systems for walls should:

a. resist the penetration of precipitation to the inside of the building; and

b. not be damaged by precipitation and not carry precipitation to any part of the building which would be damaged by it.

5.20 Cladding can be designed to protect a building from precipitation (often driven by the wind) either by holding it at the face of the building or by stopping it from penetrating beyond the back of the cladding.

5.21 Any cladding will meet the requirement if:

a. it is jointless or has sealed joints, and is impervious to moisture (so that moisture will not enter the cladding); or

b. it has overlapping dry joints, is impervious or weather resisting, and is backed by a material which will direct precipitation which enters the cladding towards the outer face.

5.22 Some materials can deteriorate rapidly without special care and they should only be used as the weather-resisting part of a cladding system if certain conditions are met (see Approved Document supporting Regulation 7, Materials and workmanship). The weather-resisting part of a cladding system does not include paint nor does it include any coating, surfacing or rendering which will not itself provide all the weather resistance.

Technical solution

5.23 Cladding may be:

a. **impervious** including metal, plastic, glass and bituminous products; or

b. **weather resisting** including natural stone or slate, cement based products, fired clay and wood; or

c. **moisture resisting** including bituminous and plastic products lapped at the joints, if used as a sheet material, and permeable to water vapour unless there is a ventilated space directly behind the material; or

d. **jointless materials** and **sealed joints**, which would allow for structural and thermal movement.

5.24 Dry joints between cladding units should be designed so that precipitation will not pass through them, or the cladding should be designed so that precipitation which enters the joints will be directed towards the exposed face without it penetrating beyond the back of the cladding.

Note: Whether dry joints are suitable will depend on the design of the joint or the design of the cladding and the severity of the exposure to wind and rain.

5.25 Each sheet, tile and section of cladding should be securely fixed. Guidance as to appropriate fixing methods is given in BS 8000-6:1990[117]. Particular care should be taken with detailing and workmanship at the junctions between cladding and window and door openings as they are vulnerable to moisture ingress.

5.26 Insulation can be incorporated into the construction provided it is either protected from moisture or unaffected by it.

5.27 Where cladding is supported by timber components or is on the façade of a timber framed building, the space between the cladding and the building should be ventilated to ensure rapid drying of any water that penetrates the cladding.

113 BRE Report BR 262 *Thermal insulation: avoiding risks*, 2002.
114 BRE Building Elements series: *Walls, windows and doors*, 2002.
115 BRE Report BR 292 *Cracking in buildings*, 1995.
116 BS 5628-3:2001 Code of practice for use of masonry. Materials and components, design and workmanship.
117 BS 8000-6:1990 Workmanship on building sites. Code of practice for slating and tiling of roofs and claddings.

Alternative approach

5.28 The requirement can also be met by following the relevant recommendations of:

a. BS CP 143[118] for sheet roof and wall coverings made from the following materials:

Part 1:1958 Corrugated and troughed aluminium

Part 5:1964 Zinc

Part 10:1973 Galvanised corrugated steel

Part 12:1970 (1988) Copper

Part 15:1973 (1986) Aluminium

Part 16:1974 Semi-rigid asbestos bitumen sheets

Recommendations for lead are included in BS 6915:2001[119];

b. BS 8219:2001[120];

c. BS 8200:1985[121];

d. BS 8297:2000[122];

e. BS 8298:1994[123];

f. MCRMA Technical Paper 6 [124];

g. MCRMA Technical Paper 9 [125].

These documents describe the materials and contain design considerations including recommendations for fixing.

JOINT BETWEEN DOORS AND WINDOWS

5.29 The joint between walls and door and window frames should:

a. resist the penetration of precipitation to the inside of the building; and

b. not be damaged by precipitation and not permit precipitation to reach any part of the building which would be damaged by it.

5.30 Damp-proof courses should be provided to direct moisture towards the outside:

a. where the downward flow of moisture would be interrupted at an obstruction, e.g. at a lintel;

b. where sill elements, including joints, do not form a complete barrier to the transfer of precipitation, e.g. under openings, windows and doors;

c. where reveal elements, including joints, do not form a complete barrier to the transfer of rain and snow, e.g. at openings, windows and doors.

5.31 In some cases the width of the cavity due to thermal insulation and the 50mm clearance for drainage may be such that the window frame is not wide enough to completely cover the cavity closer. The reveal may need to be lined with plasterboard, dry lining, a support system or a thermal backing board. Direct plastering of the internal reveal should only be used with a backing of expanded metal lathing or similar.

5.32 In areas of the country in driving rain exposure zone 4 checked rebates should be used in all window and door reveals. The frame should be set back behind the outer leaf of masonry, which should overlap it as shown in Diagram 13. Alternatively an insulated finned cavity closer may be used.

Diagram 13 **Window reveals for use in areas of severe or very severe exposure to driving rain (see paragraph 5.32)**

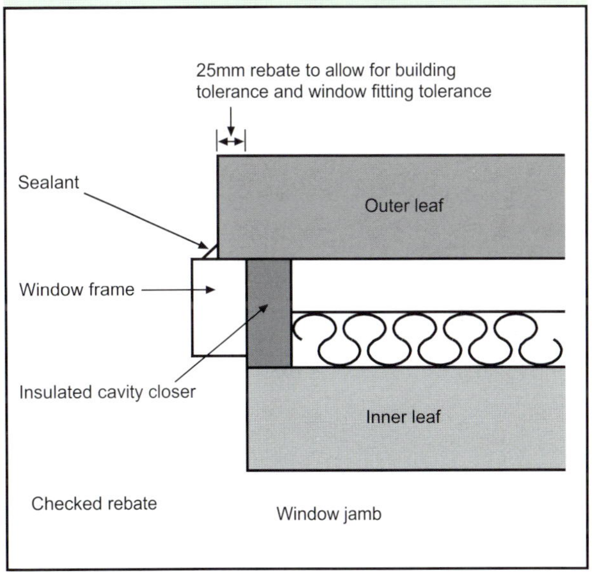

DOOR THRESHOLDS

5.33 Where an accessible threshold is provided to allow unimpeded access, as specified in Part M, Access to and use of buildings, it will meet the requirement if:

118 BS CP 143 Code of practice for sheet roof and wall coverings.

119 BS 6915:2001 Design and construction of fully supported lead sheet roof and wall coverings. Code of practice.

120 BS 8219:2001 Installation of sheet roof and wall coverings. Profiled fibre cement. Code of practice.

121 BS 8200:1985 Code of practice for the design of nonloadbearing external vertical enclosures of buildings.

122 BS 8297:2000 Code of practice for design and installation of non-loadbearing precast concrete cladding.

123 BS 8298:1994 Code of practice for design and installation of natural stone cladding and lining.

124 MCRMA Technical Paper 6 *Profiled metal roofing design guide*, revised edition, 1996.

125 MCRMA Technical Paper 9 *Composite roof and wall cladding panel design guide*, 1995.

Diagram 14 **Accessible threshold for use in exposed areas[128] (see paragraph 5.33)**

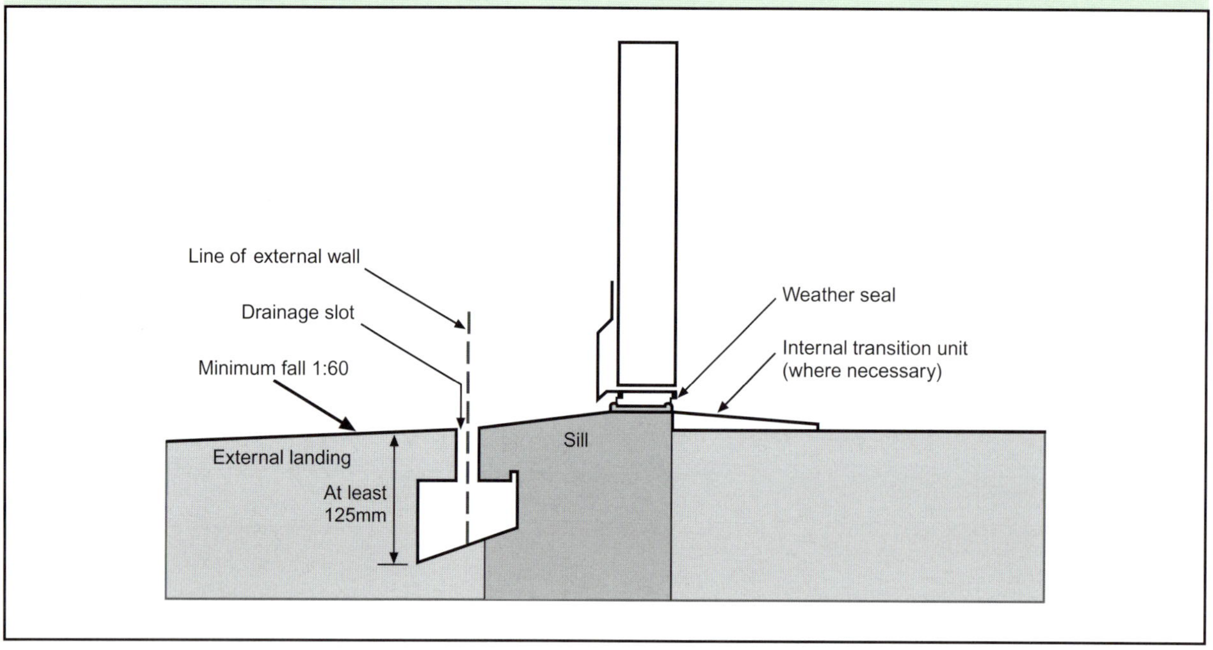

a. the external landing (Diagram 14) is laid to a fall between 1 in 40 and 1 in 60 in a single direction away from the doorway;

b. the sill leading up to the door threshold has a maximum slope of 15°.

Further advice for the development of accessible thresholds is given in BRE GBG 47[126] and the TSO document[127].

EXTERNAL WALLS (RESISTANCE TO DAMAGE FROM INTERSTITIAL CONDENSATION)

5.34 An external wall will meet the requirement if it is designed and constructed in accordance with Clause 8.3 of BS 5250:2002[129], and BS EN ISO 13788:2001[130].

5.35 Because of the high internal temperatures and humidities, there is a particular risk of interstitial condensation in the walls of swimming pools and other buildings in which high levels of moisture are generated; specialist advice should be sought when these are being designed.

EXTERNAL WALLS (RESISTANCE TO SURFACE CONDENSATION AND MOULD GROWTH)

5.36 An external wall will meet the requirement if:

a. it is designed and constructed so that the thermal transmittance (U-value) does not exceed 0.7W/m^{2}K at any point; and

b. the junctions between elements and details of openings, such as doors and windows, are designed in accordance with the recommendations in the report on robust construction details[131], or follow the guidance of BRE IP17/01[132].

---

126 BRE GBG 47 *Level external thresholds: reducing moisture penetration and thermal bridging*, 2001.

127 *Accessible thresholds in new buildings: guidance for house builders and designers*, TSO, 1999.

128 The drainage channel and adjacent paving and threshold are usually made up from precast concrete or other pre-formed components.

129 BS 5250:2002 Code of practice for the control of condensation in buildings.

130 BS EN ISO 13788:2001 Hygrothermal performance of building components and building elements. Internal surface temperature to avoid critical surface humidity and interstitial condensation. Calculation methods.

131 *Limiting thermal bridging and air leakage: robust construction details for dwellings and similar buildings*, TSO, 2001.

132 BRE Information Paper IP17/01 *Assessing the effects of thermal bridging at junctions and around openings*, 2001.

Section 6: Roofs

6.1 This section gives guidance for three situations:

a. roofs exposed to precipitation from the outside (see paragraphs 6.3 to 6.9);

b. the risk of interstitial condensation in roofs (see paragraphs 6.10 to 6.13);

c. the risk of condensation or mould growth on the internal surface of roofs (see paragraph 6.14).

6.2 Roofs should:

a. resist the penetration of precipitation to the inside of the building; and

b. not be damaged by precipitation and not carry precipitation to any part of the building which would be damaged by it;

c. be designed and constructed so that their structural and thermal performance are not adversely affected by interstitial condensation.

ROOFS (RESISTANCE TO MOISTURE FROM THE OUTSIDE)

6.3 Roofing can be designed to protect a building from precipitation either by holding the precipitation at the face of the roof or by stopping it from penetrating beyond the back of the roofing system.

6.4 Any roof will meet the requirement if:

a. it is jointless or has sealed joints, and is impervious to moisture (so that moisture will not enter the roofing system); or

b. it has overlapping dry joints, is impervious or weather resisting, and is backed by a material which will direct precipitation which enters the roof towards the outer face (as with roofing felt).

6.5 Some materials can deteriorate rapidly without special care and they should only be used as the weather-resisting part of a roof if certain conditions are met (see Approved Document supporting Regulation 7, Materials and workmanship[133]). The weather-resisting part of a roofing system does not include paint nor does it include any coating, surfacing or rendering which will not itself provide all the weather resistance.

Technical solution

6.6 Roofing systems may be:

a. **impervious** including metal, plastic and bituminous products; or

b. **weather resisting** including natural stone or slate, cement based products, fired clay and wood; or

c. **moisture resisting** including bituminous and plastic products lapped at the joints, if used as a sheet material, and permeable to water vapour unless there is a ventilated space directly behind the material; or

d. **jointless materials** and **sealed joints**, which would allow for structural and thermal movement.

6.7 Dry joints between roofing sheets should be designed so that precipitation will not pass through them, or the system should be designed so that precipitation which enters the joints will be drained away without penetrating beyond the back of the roofing system. **Note: Whether dry joints are suitable will depend on the design of the joint or the design of the roofing system and the severity of the exposure to wind and rain.**

6.8 Each sheet, tile and section of roof should be fixed in an appropriate manner. Guidance as to appropriate fixing methods is given in BS 8000-6:1990[134].

Alternative approach

6.9 The requirement can also be met by following the relevant recommendations of:

a. BS CP 143[135] for sheet roof and wall coverings made from the following materials:

Part 1:1958 *Corrugated and troughed aluminium*

Part 5:1964 Zinc

Part 10:1973 Galvanized corrugated steel

Part 12:1970 (1988) Copper

Part 15:1973 (1986) Aluminium

Part 16:1974 Semi-rigid asbestos bitumen sheets.

Recommendations for lead are included in BS 6915:2001[136];

b. BS 8219:2001[137];

c. BS 8200:1985[138];

---

133 Approved Document to support Regulation 7: Materials and workmanship, ODPM, 1998 edition (amended 2000).

134 BS 8000-6:1990 Workmanship on building sites. Code of practice for slating and tiling of roofs and claddings.

135 BS CP 143 Code of practice for sheet roof and wall coverings.

136 BS 6915:2001 Design and construction of fully supported lead sheet roof and wall coverings. Code of practice.

137 BS 8219:2001 Installation of sheet roof and wall coverings. Profiled fibre cement. Code of practice.

138 BS 8200:1985 Code of practice for the design of nonloadbearing external vertical enclosures of buildings.

d. MCRMA Technical Paper 6[139];

e. MCRMA Technical Paper 9[140].

These documents describe the materials and contain design considerations including recommendations for fixing.

ROOFS (RESISTANCE TO DAMAGE FROM INTERSTITIAL CONDENSATION)

6.10 A roof will meet the requirement if it is designed and constructed in accordance with Clause 8.4 of BS 5250:2002[141] and BS EN ISO 13788:2002[142]. Further guidance is given in the BRE Report BR 262[143].

6.11 The requirement will be met by the ventilation of cold deck roofs, i.e. those roofs where the moisture from the building can permeate the insulation. For the purposes of health and safety it may not always be necessary to provide ventilation to small roofs such as those over porches and bay windows. Although a part of a roof which has a pitch of 70° or more is to be insulated as though it were a wall, the provisions in this document apply to roofs of any pitch.

6.12 To avoid excessive moisture transfer to roof voids gaps and penetrations for pipes and electrical wiring should be filled and sealed; this is particularly important in areas of high humidity, e.g. bathrooms and kitchens. An effective draught seal should be provided to loft hatches to reduce inflow of warm air and moisture.

6.13 Because of the high internal temperatures and humidities, there is a particular risk of interstitial condensation in the roofs of swimming pools and other buildings in which high levels of moisture are generated; specialist advice should be sought when these are being designed.

ROOFS (RESISTANCE TO SURFACE CONDENSATION AND MOULD GROWTH)

6.14 A roof will meet the requirement if:

a. it is designed and constructed so that the thermal transmittance (U-value) does not exceed 0.35W/m2K at any point; and

b. the junctions between elements and the details of openings, such as windows, are designed in accordance with the recommendations in the report on robust construction details144, or follow the guidance of BRE IP17/01145 or MCRMA Paper 14146 for profiled metal roofing.

---

139 MCRMA Technical Paper 6 *Profiled metal roofing design guide*, revised edition, 1996.

140 MCRMA Technical Paper 9 *Composite roof and wall cladding panel design guide*, 1995.

141 BS 5250:2002 Code of practice for the control of condensation in buildings.

142 BS EN ISO 13788:2002 Hygrothermal performance of building components and building elements. Internal surface temperature to avoid critical surface humidity and interstitial condensation. Calculation methods.

143 BRE Report BR 262 *Thermal insulation: avoiding risks*, 2002.

144 *Limiting thermal bridging and air leakage: robust construction details for dwellings and similar buildings*, DTLR, 2001.

145 BRE Information Paper IP17/01 *Assessing the effects of thermal bridging at junctions and around openings*, 2001.

146 MCRMA Technical Paper 14 *Guidance for the design of metal roofing and cladding to comply with approved document L2:2001*, 2002.

British Standards referred to

[3] **BS 7913:1998**
Guide to the principles of the conservation of historic buildings.

[14,36] **BS 5930:1999**
Code of practice for site investigations.

[21] **BS 8103-1:1995**
Structural design of low-rise buildings. Code of practice for stability, site investigation, foundations and ground floor slabs for housing. AMD 8980 1995.

[37] **BS 10175:2001**
Investigation of potentially contaminated sites. Code of practice.

[48] **BS 3882:1994**
Specification for topsoil. AMD 9938 1998.

[84,89] **BS 8500-1:2002**
Concrete. Complementary British Standard to BS EN 206-1. Method of specifying and guidance for the specifier.
AMD 14639 2003.

[86] **BS 1282:1999**
Wood preservatives. Guidance on choice, use and application.

[87,94] **CP 102:1973**
Code of practice for protection of buildings against water from the ground.
AMD 1551 1974, AMD 2196 1977,
AMD 2470 1978.

[88,102] **BS 8102:1990**
Code of practice for protection of structures against water from the ground.

BS 5628-3:2001
Code of practice for use of masonry. Materials and components, design and workmanship.

[91] **BS 7331:1990**
Specification for direct surfaced wood chipboard based on thermosetting resins.
AMD 8537 1995.
(Withdrawn.)

[92] **BS EN 312-5:1997**
Particleboards. Specifications. Requirements for load-bearing boards for use in humid conditions.
(Withdrawn and superseded by BS EN 312:2003 Particle boards. Specifications.)

[96,129,141] **BS 5250:2002**
Code of practice for the control of condensation in buildings.

[97,130,142] **BS EN ISO 3788:2002**
Hygrothermal performance of building components and building elements. Internal surface temperature to avoid critical surface humidity and interstitial condensation. Calculation methods. AMD 13792 2002.

[101] **BS 8215:1991**
Code of practice for design and installation of damp-proof courses in masonry construction.

[103,112] **BS 8104:1992**
Code of practice for assessing exposure of walls to wind-driven rain. AMD 8358 1995.

[105] **BS EN 998-2:2003**
Specification for mortar for masonry. Masonry mortar.

[106] **BS 5262:1991**
Code of practice for external renderings.

[109] **BS 5617:1985**
Specification for ureaformaldehyde (UF) foam systems suitable for thermal insulation of cavity walls with masonry or concrete inner and outer leaves.

[110] **BS 5618:1985**
Code of practice for thermal insulation of cavity walls (with masonry or concrete inner and outer leaves) by filling with urea-formaldehyde (UF) foam systems.
AMD 6262 1990, AMD 7114 1992.

[111] **BS 8208-1:1985**
Guide to assessment of suitability of external cavity walls for filling with thermal insulants. Existing traditional cavity construction. AMD 4996 1985.

[117,134] **BS 8000-6:1990**
Workmanship on building sites. Code of practice for slating and tiling of roofs and claddings.

[118,135] **CP 143-1:1958**
Code of practice for sheet roof and wall coverings. Aluminium, corrugated and troughed. Amended by PD 4346 1961.
(Obsolescent.)

[118,135] **CP 143-5:1964**
Code of practice for sheet roof and wall coverings. Code of practice for sheet roof and wall coverings. Zinc.

[118,135] **CP 143-10:1973**
Code of practice for sheet roof and wall coverings. Code of practice for sheet roof and wall coverings. Galvanized corrugated steel. Metric units.

[118,135] **CP 143-12:1970**
Code of practice for sheet roof and wall coverings. Code of practice for sheet roof and wall coverings. Copper. Metric units.

[118,135] **CP 143-15:1973**
Code of practice for sheet roof and wall coverings. Code of practice for sheet roof and wall coverings. Aluminium. Metric units.
AMD 4473 1984.

[118,135] **CP 143-16:1974**
Code of practice for sheet roof and wall coverings. Code of practice for sheet roof and wall coverings. Semi-rigid asbestos bitumen sheet. Metric units.
(Withdrawn in 2004.)

[119,136] **BS 6915:2001**
Design and construction of fully supported lead sheet roof and wall coverings.
Code of practice.

[120,137] **BS 8219:2001**
Installation of sheet roof and wall coverings. Profiled fibre cement. Code of practice.

[121,138] **BS 8200:1985**
Code of practice for the design of non-loadbearing external vertical enclosures of buildings.
(Obsolescent.)

[122] **BS 8297:2000**

Code of practice for design and installation of non-loadbearing precast concrete cladding. AMD 11064 2000,
AMD 13018 2000.

[123] **BS 8298:1994**

Code of practice for design and installation of natural stone cladding and lining.

British Standards available from: BSI, PO Box 6206, Chiswick, London, W4 4ZL. Website: www.bsonline.techindex.co.uk

C Other documents referred to

Arup Environmental

[78] DETR/Arup Environmental Partners in Technology (PIT) Research Report: *Passive venting of soil gases beneath buildings*, Volume 1: *Guide for design* & Volume 2: *Guide for design – computational fluid dynamics modelling: example output*, 1997.

Available to download from:
Volume 1: www.arup.com/DOWNLOADBANK/download133.pdf
Volume 2: www.cordek.co.uk/pdf/vent_vol2.pdf
Website: www.arup.com

Association of Geotechnical and Geoenvironmental Specialists (AGS)

[35] *Guidelines for combined geoenvironmental and geotechnical investigations*, 2000.

Available from AGS, Forum Court, 83 Coopers Cope Road, Beckenham, Kent, BR3 1NR. Website: www.ags.org.uk.

British Geological Survey (BGS)

[63] BGS Technical Report WP 95/1 *Methane, carbon dioxide and oil seeps from natural sources and mining areas: characteristics, extent and relevance to planning and development in Great Britain*, 1995. ISBN X 78089 337 8

Available from BGS Sales Desk, Keyworth, Nottingham, NB12 5GG.
Website: www.bgs.ac.uk.

BRE

Digest 240 *Low-rise buildings on shrinkable clay soils*: Part 1, 1993. ISBN 0 85125 609 0

[23] Digest 241 Low-rise buildings on shrinkable clay soils: Part 2, 1990. ISBN 0 85125 377 6

[24] BRE Digest 242 Low-rise buildings on shrinkable clay soils: Part 3, 1993.

[83] Digest 276 Hardcore, 1992. ISBN 0 85125 316 4

[22] Digest 298 *Low-rise building foundations: the influence of trees in clay soils*, 1999. ISBN 1 86081 278 3

[16] Digest 318 *Site investigation for low-rise building: desk studies*, 1987. ISBN 0 85125 240 0

[15] Digest 322 *Site investigation for low-rise building: procurement*, 1987. ISBN 0 85125 254 0

[17] Digest 348 *Site investigation for low-rise building: the walk-over survey*, 1989. ISBN 0 85125 424 1

[18] Digest 381 *Site investigation for low-rise building: trial pits*, 1993. ISBN 0 85125 570 1

[19] Digest 383 *Site investigation for low-rise building: soil description*, 1993. ISBN 0 85125 596 5

[20] Digest 411 *Site investigation for low-rise building: direct investigations*, 1995. ISBN 1 86081 061 6

[27] Digest 427 *Low-rise buildings on fill: classification and load-carrying characteristics: Part 1*, 1997. ISBN 1 86081 190 6

[27] Digest 427 *Low-rise buildings on fill: site investigation, ground movement and foundation design: Part 2*, 1998. ISBN 1 86081 191 4

[27] Digest 427 *Low-rise buildings on fill: engineered fill: Part 3*, 1998. ISBN 1 86081 192 2

[93] Digest 429 *Timbers: their natural durability and resistance to preservative treatment*, 1998. ISBN 1 86081 209 0

[6,78] Good Building Guide 25 *Buildings and radon*, 1996. ISBN 1 86081 070 5

[126] Good Building Guide 47 *Level external thresholds: reducing moisture penetration and thermal bridging*, 2001. ISBN 1 86081 488 3

[100,132,145] Information Paper 17/01 *Assessing the effects of thermal bridging at junctions around openings*, 2001. ISBN 1 86081 506 5

[75,81] Report 211 *Radon: guidance on protective measures for new dwellings*, 1999. ISBN 1 86081 328 3

[98,113,143] Report 262 *Thermal insulation: avoiding risks*, 2002. ISBN 1 86081 515 4

[5] Report 267 *Major alterations and conversions: a BRE guide to radon remedial actions in existing buildings*, 1994. ISBN 0 85125 638 4

[115] Report 292 *Cracking in buildings*, 1996. ISBN 1 86081 039 X

[77] Report 293 *Radon in the workplace*, 1995. ISBN 1 86081 040 3

[114] Report 352 *BRE Building elements: walls, windows and doors – performance, diagnosis, maintenance, repair and the avoidance of defects*, 1998. ISBN 1 86081 235 X

[74,80] Report 414 *Protective measures for housing on gas-contaminated land*, 2001. ISBN 1 86081 460 3

[28] Report 424 *Building on fill: geotechnical aspects. 2nd edition*, 2001. ISBN 1 86081 509 X

[33,85] Special Digest 1 *Concrete in aggressive ground: assessing the aggressive chemical environment: Part 1*, 2001 (Amended 2003). ISBN 1 86081 502 2

[33,85] Special Digest 1 *Concrete in aggressive ground: specifying concrete and additional protective measures: Part 2*, 2001 (Amended 2003). ISBN 1 86081 503 0

[33,85] Special Digest 1 *Concrete in aggressive ground: design guides for common applications: Part 3*, 2001 (Amended 2003). ISBN 1 86081 504 9

[33,85] Special Digest 1 *Concrete in aggressive ground: design guides for specific precast products: Part 4*, 2001 (Amended 2003). ISBN 1 86081 505 7

Available from: BREbookshop, Bucknalls Lane, Garston, Watford, WD25 9XX Tel 01344 404407. Website: www.brebookshop.com. Email: bookshop@bre.co.uk.

Chartered Institution of Wastes Management (CIWM)

[61] *Monitoring of landfill gas*, 2nd edition, 1998.

Available from CIWM Publications Department, 9 Saxon Court, St Peter's Gardens, Northampton, Northamptonshire, NN1 1SX. Website: www.ciwm.co.uk.

Construction Industry Research and Information Association (CIRIA)

[79] Publication C506 *Low-cost options for prevention of flooding from sewers*, 1998. ISBN 0 86017 506 5

[65] Report 130 *Methane: its occurrence and hazards in construction*, 1993. ISBN 0 86017 373 9

[66] Report 131 *Measurement of methane and other gases from the ground*, 1993. ISBN 0 86017 372 0

[47] Report 132 *A guide for safe working on contaminated sites*, 1996. ISBN 0 86017 451 4

[72] Report 149 *Protecting development from methane: methane and associated hazards to construction*, 1995. ISBN 0 86017 410 7

[67] Report 150 *Methane investigation strategies: methane and associated hazards to construction*, 1995. ISBN 0 86017 435 2

[68] Report 151 *Interpreting measurements of gas in the ground: methane and associated hazards to construction*, 1995. ISBN 0 86017 435 2

[69] Report 152 *Risk assessment for methane and other gases from the ground: methane and associated hazards to construction*, 1995. ISBN 0 86017 434 4

[50] Special Publication SP102 *Remedial treatment for contaminated land: Volume II: decommissioning, decontamination and demolition*, 1995. ISBN 0 86017 397 6

[51] Special Publication SP104 *Remedial treatment for contaminated land: Volume IV: classification and selection of remedial methods*, 1995. ISBN 0 86017 339 2

[52] Special Publication SP105 *Remedial treatment for contaminated land: Volume V: excavation and disposal*, 1995. ISBN 0 86017 400 X

[53] Special Publication SP106 *Remedial treatment for contaminated land: Volume VI: containment and hydraulic measures*, 1996. ISBN 0 86017 401 8

[54] Special Publication SP107 *Remedial treatment for contaminated land: Volume VII: ex-situ remedial methods for soils, sludges and sediments*, 1995. ISBN 0 86017 402 6

[55] Special Publication SP109 *Remedial treatment for contaminated land: Volume IX: in-situ methods of remediation*, 1995. ISBN 0 86017 404 2

[49] Special Publication SP124 *Barriers liners and cover systems for containment and control of land contamination*, 1996. ISBN 0 86017 437 9

Available from CIRIA, Classic House, 174-180 Old Street, London, EC1V 9BP. Website: www.ciria.org/index.html. Tel: 020 7549 3300. Email: enquiries@ciria.org.

CIRIA/Environment Agency

[10] CIRIA/Environment Agency *Flood products: using flood protection products - a guide for homeowners, 2003.*

Available to download from www.environment-agency.gov.uk/subjects/flood/826674/882909/483622/484713/?version=1&lang=_e.

Website: www.ciria.org.

Department for Transport, Local Government and the Regions (DTLR)

[7] Planning Policy Guidance Note PPG 25 *Development and flood risk*, 2001.

Available to download from www.odpm.gov.uk/index.aspfiid=1144115#P21_904.

[99,131,144] *Limiting thermal bridging and air leakage: robust construction details for dwellings and similar buildings*, 2002. ISBN 0 11 753631 8

Department of the Environment (DoE)

[12] Planning Policy Guidance Note PPG 23: *Planning and pollution control*, 1997. (Superseded by ODPM Planning Policy Statement 23: *Planning and pollution control*, 2004.)

Available to download from www.odpm.gov.uk/index.aspfiid=1143919#.)

[29] 47 Industry profiles, 1995-1996.

Available to download from www.environment-agency.gov.uk/subjects/landquality/113813/1166435/?version=1&lang=_e.

[64] *Methane and other gases from disused coal mines: the planning response*, 1996. ISBN 0 11753 307 6 (Out of print.)

Waste Management Paper No 27 Landfill gas, 2nd edition, 1991. (Replaced by Environment Agency LFTGN 03 *Guidance on the management of landfill gas*, 2004. Available to download from www.environment-agency.gov.uk/commondata/105385/lf_tgn_03_888494.pdf.)

DEFRA/Environment Agency

[39] Contaminated Land Research Report CLR 7 *Assessment of risks to human health from land contamination: an overview of the development of soil guideline values and related research*, 2002. ISBN 1 85705 732 5

[30,40] Contaminated Land Research Report CLR 8 *Potential contaminants for the assessment of land*, 2002. ISBN 1 85705 733 3

[41] Contaminated Land Research Report CLR 9 *Contaminants in soil: collation of toxicological data and intake values for humans*, 2002. ISBN 1 85705 734 1

[42] Contaminated *Land Research Report CLR 10 Contaminated land exposure assessment (CLEA) model: technical basis and algorithms*, 2002. ISBN 1 85705 749 X

Available to download from www.environment-agency.gov.uk/subjects/landquality/113813/672771/675330/?version=1&lang=_e.

[43,71] Contaminated Land Research Report CLR 11 *Model procedures for the management of land contamination*, 2004. ISBN 1 84432 295 5

Available to download from http://publications.environment-agency.gov.uk/epages/eapublications.storefront/43cbc16a013ad26e2740c0a8029606d2/Product/View/SCHO0804BIBR&2DE&2DE.

Environment Agency

LFTGN 03 *Guidance on the management of landfill gas*, 2004.

Available to download from www.environment-agency.gov.uk commondata/105385/lf_tgn_03_888494.pdf.

[38] National Groundwater & Contaminated Land Centre Report NC/99/38/2 *Guide to good practice for the development of conceptual models and the selection and application of mathematical models of contaminant transport processes in the subsurface*, 2001. ISBN 1 85705 610 8

Available to download from http://publications.environment-agency.gov.uk/epages/eapublications.storefront/43cbbad2010802c62740c0a80296064a/Product/View/SCHO0701BITR&2DE&2DE.

[59] R & D Technical Report P5-035/TR/01 *Assessment and management of risks to buildings, building materials and services from land contamination*, 2001. ISBN 1 85705 484 9

Available to download from http://publications.environment-agency.gov.uk/pdf/SP5-035-TR-1-e-p.pdf.

[44] R & D Technical Report P5-065/TR-I *Technical aspects of site investigation.* Volume I (of II) 'Overview', 2000. ISBN 1 85705 544 6

[44] R & D Technical Report P5-065/TR-II *Technical aspects of site investigation.* Volume II (of II) 'Text supplements', 2000. ISBN 1 85705 545 4

Available to download from www.environment-agency.gov.uk/subjects/landquality/113813/887579/1103420/?version=1&lang=_e.

[45] R & D Technical Report P5-066 Secondary model procedure for the development of appropriate soil sampling strategies for land contamination, 2000. ISBN 1 85705 577 2

Available to download from http://publications.environment-agency.gov.uk/epages/eapublications.storefront/43ccb7670219a1c62740c0a8029606df/Product/View/SP5&2D066&2DTR&2DE&2DE.

[31] R & D Technical Report P291 *Information on land quality in England: Sources of information (including background contaminants)*, 2002. ISBN 1 85705 123 8

[32] R & D Technical Report P292 *Information on land quality in Wales: Sources of information (including background contaminants)*, 2002. ISBN 1 85705 124 6

Available to download from www.environment-agency.gov.uk/subjects/landquality/113813/887579/1103420/?version=1&lang=_e.

[70] Golder Associates, 2002 GasSIM (version 2) landfill gas assessment tool, a computer programme.

Available from www.gassim.co.uk.

Various Contaminated Land Research Reports (CLR), Soil Guideline Values (SGV) and Toxicological Reports (TOX) are available to download from www.environment-agency.gov.uk/subjects/landquality/113813/672771/675330/fiversion=1&lang=_e.

Foundation for the Built Environment (FBE)
(now known as the BRE Trust)

Subsidence damage to domestic buildings: lessons learned and questions remaining, 2000. ISBN 1 86081 433 6

Website: www.bretrust.org.uk

Available from BREbookshop, Bucknalls Lane, Garston, Watford, WD25 9XX. Website: www.brebookshop.com. Tel 01344 404407. Email: bookshop@bre.co.uk.

Foundation for Water Research (FWR)

[58] Report FR0448 Laying potable water pipelines in contaminated ground: guidance notes, 1994.

Available from FWR, Allen House, The Listons, Liston Road, Marlow, Bucks SL7 1FD. Website: www.fwr.org. Tel: 01628 8911589.

Health and Safety Executive (HSE)

[46] HSG 66 *Protection of workers and the general public during the development of contaminated land*, 1991. ISBN 0 11885 857 X

Available from HSE Books, PO Box 1999, Sudbury, Suffolk, CO10 2WA. Website: www.hsebooks.com. Tel: 01787 881165.

Institute of Petroleum (IP)
(now the Energy Institute, created in 2003 by the merger of the Institute of Petroleum and the Institute of Energy)

[62] TP 95 *Guidelines for investigation and remediation of petroleum retail sites*, 1998. ISBN 0 85293 216 2

Available from Portland Customer Services, Portland Press Ltd, Commerce Way, Whitehall Industrial Estate, Colchester, CO2 8HP. Website: www. energyinst.org.uk. Tel: 01206 796351.
E-mail: sales@portland-services.com.

Metal Cladding and Roofing Manufacturers Association (MCRMA)

[124,139] MCRMA Technical Paper 6 *Profiled metal roofing design guide, revised edition*, 1996. (Superseded by the 2004 edition.)

[125,140] MCRMA Technical Paper 9 *Composite roof and wall cladding panel design guide*, 1995.

[146] MCRMA Technical Paper 14 *Guidance for the design of metal roofing and cladding to comply with Approved Document L2*: 2001, 2002.

Available from MCRMA Ltd, 18 Mere Farm Road, Prenton, Wirral, Cheshire, CH43 9TT. Website www.mcrma.co.uk. Tel: 0151 652 3846. Email: mcrma@ compuserve.com.

National House-Building Council (NHBC)

[26] NHBC Standards Chapter 4.2 Building near trees, 2003 + (2005 Amendment).

Available from NHBC, Buildmark House, Chiltern Avenue, Amersham, Bucks HP6 5AP. Website: www.nhbcbuilder.co.uk. Tel: 01494 735363. Email: cssupport@nhbc.co.uk.

Office of the Deputy Prime Minister (ODPM)

[12] Planning Policy Statement 23: *Planning and pollution control*, 2004.

Available to download from www.odpm.gov.uk/index.aspfiid=1143919#.

[8,56,95] *Preparing for floods: interim guidance for improving the flood resistance of domestic and small business properties*, 2002. (Reprinted with amendments 2003.)

Available to download from www.odpm.gov.uk.

[133] Approved Document to support Regulation 7: Materials and workmanship, 1999.

Available to download from www.odpm.gov.uk/index.aspfiid=1130911.

Society for the Protection of Ancient Buildings (SPAB)

[4] Information Sheet 4 *The need for old buildings to 'breathe'*, 1986.

Available from The Society for the Protection of Ancient Buildings, 37 Spital Square, London, E1 6DY. Website: www.spab.org.uk. Tel: 020 7377 1644. Email: info@spab.org.uk.

Scottish Office (SO)

[9,57] *Design guidance on flood damage to dwellings*, 1996. ISBN 0 11495 776 2

The Stationery Office (TSO)

[127] *Accessible thresholds in new buildings. Guidance for house builders and designers*, 1999. ISBN 0 11702 333 7

Annex A: Guidance on the assessment of land affected by contaminants

A.1 A substantial amount of guidance on the assessment of contaminated land has been published to support the implementation of Part IIA of the Environmental Protection Act 1991. Most of this guidance is contained in the joint Defra/Environment Agency Contaminated Land Research Reports (CLRs). This guidance can be used to support the assessment process set out in Section 2. A summary of the reports is set out below and an outline of the process is given in Figure A1[147].

A.2 For health, risk estimation can be carried out using generic assessment criteria such as contaminant soil guideline values (SGVs) or relevant and appropriate environmental standards. SGVs represent contaminant concentrations which may pose unacceptable risks to health. The development of SGVs for a range of priority contaminants is described in the Defra/ Environment Agency reports CLR 7[148], CLR 8[149], CLR 9[150] and CLR 10[151].

A.3 CLR 10 describes the Contaminated Land Exposure Assessment Model (CLEA) for deriving SGVs for three different site uses: (i) residential, (ii) residential with plant uptake and (iii) commercial/industrial. In this way the relative importance of each of the pollutant linkages is considered. For example, for residential site use it is assumed residents have private gardens and/ or access to community open space close to the home and that some may use their gardens to grow vegetables. CLR 10 gives details of the conceptual model underpinning each of the standard land uses.

A.4 A series of Defra/Environment Agency SGV reports[152] contain SGVs for a range of contaminants, one report for each contaminant, and the corresponding TOX reports[153] contain the toxicological data used to derive the SGVs. SGVs should be used only in conjunction with the CLR 7 to 10 reports and associated SGV and TOX reports.

A.5 The use of ICRCL (Interdepartmental Committee on the Redevelopment of Contaminated Land) document *Guidance Note 59/83: Guidance on the assessment and redevelopment of contaminated land*[154] is no longer appropriate in health risk assessment and has been withdrawn[155] by Defra.

A.6 CLR 7 provides advice regarding such issues. In certain cases the most appropriate action may be to redesign the building layout. Further guidance can be obtained from the Environment Agency/NHBC R & D Publication 66[156].

A.7 An alternative to the generic approach is to undertake a more site-specific quantitative risk assessment using the principles of risk assessment or a risk assessment model. Specialist advice should be sought.

REFERENCES TO ANNEX A

Department for the Environment, Food and Rural Affairs (DEFRA)

[155] Contaminated land Advice *Note CLAN 3/02 Note on the withdrawal of ICRCL trigger value*, 2002.

Available to download from www.defra.gov.uk/environment/land/contaminated/pdf/clan3-02.pdf.

DEFRA/Environment Agency

[148] Contaminated Land Research Report CLR 7 *Assessment of risks to human health from land contamination: an overview of the development of soil guideline values and related research*, 2002. ISBN 1 85705 732 5

[149] Contaminated Land Research Report CLR 8 *Potential contaminants for the assessment of land*, 2002. ISBN 1 85705 733 3

[150] Contaminated Land Research Report CLR 9 *Contaminants in soil: collation of toxicological data and intake values for humans*, 2002. ISBN 1 85705 734 1

[151] Contaminated Land Research Report CLR 10 *Contaminated land exposure assessment (CLEA) model: technical basis and algorithms*, 2002. ISBN 1 85705 749 X

Available to download from www.environment-agency.gov.uk/subjects/landquality/113813/672771/675330/fiversion=1&lang=_e.

[147] Contaminated Land Research Report CLR 11 *Model procedures for the management of land contamination*, 2004. ISBN 1 84432 295 5

Available to download from http://publications.environment-agency.gov.uk/epages/eapublications.storefront/43cbc16a013ad26e2740c0a8029606d2/Product/View/SCHO0804BIBR&2DE&2DE.

[152] Soil Guideline Values (SGV) reports (separate SGV report for each contaminant), 2002.

[153] TOX reports (separate TOX report for each contaminant), 2002.

Soil Guideline Values (SGV) and Toxicological Reports (TOX) are available to download from www.environment-agency.gov.uk/subjects/landquality/113813/672771/675330/fiversion=1&lang=_e.

Environment Agency/NHBC

[156] R and D Publication 66 *Guidance for the safe development of housing on land affected by contamination*, 2000.

Available to download from http://publications.environment-agency.gov.uk/pdf/SR-DPUB66-e-e.pdf?lang=_e.

Inter-Departmental Committee on the Redevelopment of Contaminated Land (ICRCL)

[154] ICRCL Guidance Note 59/83 *Guidance on the assessment and redevelopment of contaminated land,* 2nd edition, 1987. (Withdrawn and superseded by Department for the Environment, Food and Rural Affairs (DEFRA) Contaminated land Advice Note CLAN 3/02 *Note on the withdrawal of ICRCL trigger value,* 2002 Available to download from www.defra.gov.uk/environment/land/contaminated/pdf/clan3-02.pdf.)

Diagram A1 **The process of managing land affected by contaminants**

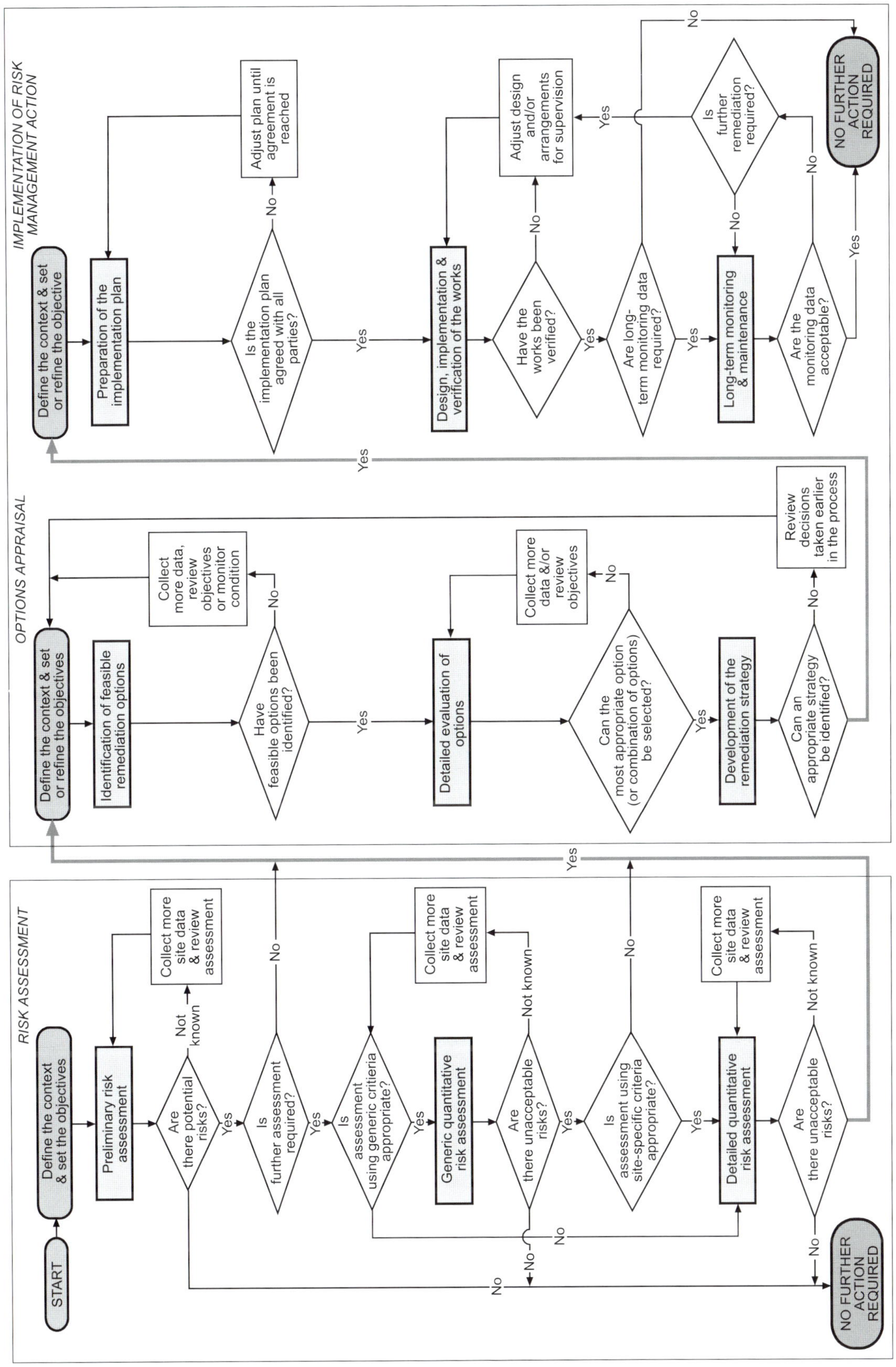

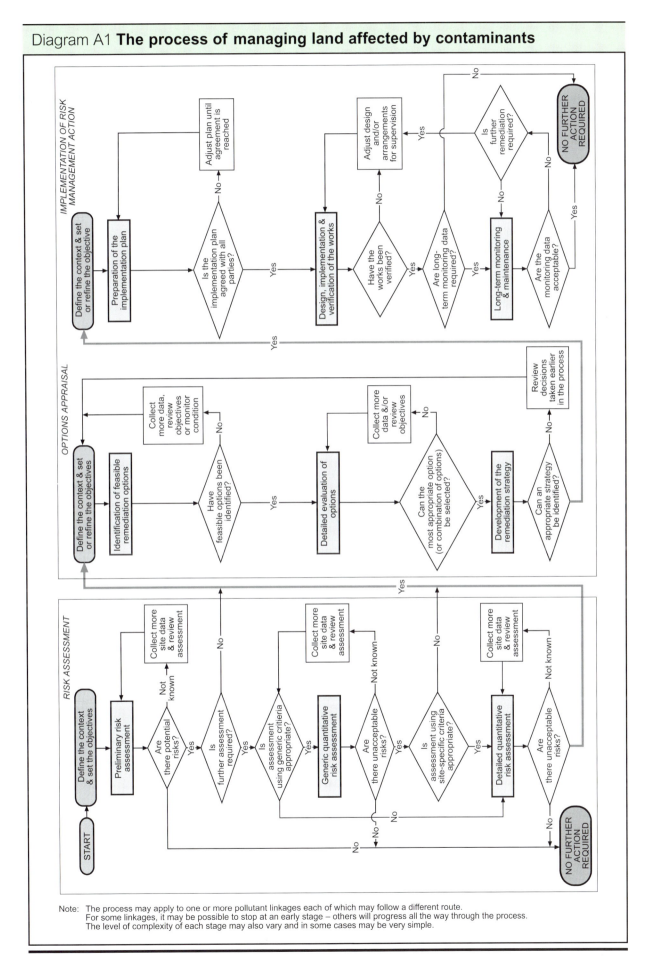

Note: The process may apply to one or more pollutant linkages each of which may follow a different route. For some linkages, it may be possible to stop at an early stage – others will progress all the way through the process. The level of complexity of each stage may also vary and in some cases may be very simple.